“Alan Ware’s account emphasises how positional
with adverse effects not only on social welfare bu
especially education. This sparkling and origin
political implications of the changing relationsh
status in contemporary Britain.”

Deborah Mabbett, *Birkbeck, University of London, UK*

“*Inequality in Britain* is an essential guide to understanding what there is to know about inequality in Britain. Alan Ware draws together the lessons of disparate fields into a comprehensive analysis of the interactions between multiple sources of inequality, demonstrating the fundamental relationships between class, gender and ethnicity. He seamlessly draws together historical perspectives and data driven economic accounts into a book that is both highly informative and a damn good read. An absolute must for the bookshelves of anyone who is concerned about who we are and what we might become.”

Rosie Campbell, *King’s College London, UK*

“What this book promises is a sketch map of how different aspects of inequality fit together. It achieves that aim admirably. But it does so much more. It shows how the development of inequality is driven by positional competition, relative deprivation and the cumulative effects of social and policy developments over time. Its concluding message – that creative political leadership is essential for an adequate set of policy responses – is both sober and ambitious. *A tour de force.*”

Albert Weale, *University College London, UK*

INEQUALITY IN BRITAIN

This book provides a thorough and engaging analysis of inequality in Britain, including its long-term development and transformation since the beginning of the 20th century.

The author argues that inequality is not what it used to be – no longer can policy-makers consider it just in terms of status, wealth and income. Having resurfaced strongly as an issue after the financial crisis of 2007–2008, a truly informed discussion of inequality must now be wide ranging and take account of a variety of interacting factors. They include both a radically different role for education in the labour market and the interests of future generations. Government policies, market failures and fundamental changes in British society and economy in earlier decades have all contributed to inequality's contemporary scope, its intensity and who it affects.

Alan Ware traces and illuminates the altered nature of inequality in Britain, its consequences and especially its political implications. It offers a timely, concise and illuminating examination that will be of interest to all those concerned about inequality and, more broadly, to scholars and students of sociology, social/public policy, contemporary British history, political sociology and political theory.

Alan Ware is an Emeritus Fellow of Worcester College, Oxford University, and a senior research associate of University College London, United Kingdom.

Routledge Studies in British Politics

Series editors: Patrick Diamond and Tim Bale
Queen Mary University, London, UK

This series aims to promote research excellence in political science, political history and public policy making, whilst addressing a wide array of political dynamics, contexts, histories and ideas. It will retain a particular focus on British government, British politics and public policy, while locating those issues within a European and global context.

Centralisation, Devolution and the Future of Local Government in England
Steve Leach, John Stewart and George Jones

The Struggle for Labour's Soul
Understanding Labour's Political Thought since 1945, second edition
Edited by Matt Beech, Kevin Hickson and Raymond Plant

British Public Opinion on Foreign and Defence Policy
1945–2017
Ben Clements

Neoliberalisms in British Politics
Christopher Byrne

The Making of the Conservative Party's Immigration Policy
Rebecca Partos

Inequality in Britain
Alan Ware

INEQUALITY IN BRITAIN

Alan Ware

LONDON AND NEW YORK

First published 2020
by Routledge
2 Park Square, Milton Park, Abingdon, Oxon OX14 4RN

and by Routledge
52 Vanderbilt Avenue, New York, NY 10017

Routledge is an imprint of the Taylor & Francis Group, an informa business

British Library Cataloguing in Publication Data
A catalogue record for this book is available from the British Library.

Library of Congress Cataloging in Publication Data
Names: Ware, Alan, author.
Title: Inequality in Britain / Alan Ware.
Description: Milton Park, Abingdon, Oxon ; New York, NY : Routledge, 2020. | Series: Routledge studies in british politics | Includes bibliographical references and index.
Identifiers: LCCN 2019028250 (print) | LCCN 2019028251 (ebook) | ISBN 9780367331603 (hardback) | ISBN 9780367331696 (paperback) | ISBN 9780429318269 (ebook)
Subjects: LCSH: Inequality—Great Britain. | Income distribution—Great Britain. | Great Britain—Economic conditions.
Classification: LCC HN400.S6 W37 2020 (print) | LCC HN400.S6 (ebook) | DDC 305.50941—dc2 3
LC record available at https://lccn.loc.gov/2019028250
LC ebook record available at https://lccn.loc.gov/2019028251

ISBN: 978-0-367-33160-3 (hbk)
ISBN: 978-0-367-33169-6 (pbk)
ISBN: 978-0-429-31826-9 (ebk)

Typeset in Bembo
by TNQ Technologies

Printed in the United Kingdom
by Henry Ling Limited

For my former students at the University of Warwick (1972–1990)
and at Worcester College, Oxford University (1990–2012).

CONTENTS

PREFACE AND ACKNOWLEDGEMENTS

There has been inequality in most human societies. How much it is discussed, or how much it dominates ideas and communications, varies both between societies and over time. Especially since the Industrial Revolution, a vast amount has been written on the subject. In Britain the subject is never entirely absent from the public domain, but how much attention we pay to it changes over time. Since the financial crisis of 2008 and during the ensuing period of austerity and low economic growth, interest in inequality, together with concern and anger about it, has grown. It might be expected, therefore, that in the English language there would be a wealth of material about inequality to which a reader could turn for an understanding of how and why high levels of inequality persist, and even grow, in affluent societies. In a sense that expectation is most certainly met – but with one important qualification.

Our knowledge of inequality, together with arguments about it, tends to be clustered around particular aspects of it, with different academic disciplines having their own versions of what is important. Partly that is because there are many diverse elements to inequality, but also because the various disciplines and sub-fields make different assumptions about evidence, modes of investigation and the direction of some causal relationships. Thus, within all the social sciences and various fields of historical studies there are many ways of focussing on inequality. The result is that we can see the equivalent of "individual trees" so clearly, but the overall shape of the "wood" in which they are located is more difficult to determine.

I spent much of my academic career engaged in research about long-term change in political parties, especially America's parties. A feature common to my work then was that many aspects of the parties' transformation since the mid-19th century had often been misunderstood, and that often many explanations academics had for it were incomplete, misleading or in some cases simply wrong. Part of the significance of received wisdoms about change is that they can badly distort how we view and understand the present. For me to explain how and why party politics had been transformed over a period of a century and more involved doing what academics are employed to do – researching the subject. And it is with major long-term change that I am concerned in this book about the bases of inequality in Britain.

Aside from the obvious point, that the subject matter of *Inequality in Britain* is dissimilar to my earlier work, the main difference between them obviously lies in the availability of evidence. Various disciplines have already engaged in such a vast amount of research on inequality that the absence of data (of various kinds) is not an issue when examining it. Instead, there is a need for linking together our knowledge of it that is to be found in a myriad of sources. What we lack, because of the breadth of the subject, is some kind of guide as to how its different elements might fit together. To use another analogy, it is not unlike being in possession of detailed maps of a country's many different regions, but a limited understanding of how all of them might link to one another. To engage in that exercise comprehensively in the case of inequality would entail writing a far longer book than this one, and one that would probably be of interest only to experts. Instead, my book resembles more a sketch of what an overall "map" might look like.

At the book's core is an attempt to explain how and why the various factors that sustained inequality at the beginning of the 20th century had been transformed within about one hundred years. In that sense, there is a continuing thread with my earlier books on political parties. Despite the wealth of material on inegalitarianism within Britain, what has happened to the processes by which inequality is maintained is only imperfectly understood. And the scale of that change has been massive. Consequently, some of the suggestions made by politicians and others as to what could be done to ease the effects of inequality are based on assumptions that just do not hold. Why Britain remains an unequal country today, although one that is grounded in different factors than it was for much of the past century, is linked to long-term developments that were, and still are, largely disregarded.

During the past decade this short book has gone through many manifestations in its gestation – longer unpublished book-length manuscripts being followed by others half their length. In this final version it has grown again. Among those friends and colleagues who kindly read and commented on earlier versions, or who talked through aspects of the subject with me over the years, I wish to thank the following: Nigel Bowles, Dan Gibton, Clare Lee, Ross Lee, Joni Lovenduski, Deborah Mabbett, Jeremy Parsons, Lindsay Paterson, Andrew Reeve and Albert Weale. In addition, Bill Jones was both enthusiastic about one of the later drafts and was also of great importance in putting me in contact with Routledge. I wish to thank the Politics Editor there, Andrew Taylor, and also Sophie Iddamalgoda, as well as two of the Press's anonymous referees for their helpful comments.

Previously I had received useful comments from another anonymous source, and without the assistance of all of the above the book would not possess whatever merits, if any, it might turn out to possess. As always, the errors and so on are my responsibility alone.

Alan Ware

June 2019

1

INTRODUCTION

In a radio broadcast during the Great Depression, the humourist and political commentator Will Rogers made the following observation about America:

> Here we are in a country with more wheat, and more corn, more money in the banks, and more cotton, more everything in the world... yet we've got people starving. We'll hold the distinction of being the only nation in the history of the world that ever went to the poor house in an automobile.

His remark of 1931 illustrates well an important aspect of inequality in all modern societies. Deprivation for a large minority can exist alongside overall abundance. In real terms, average income per head in Britain is about three times higher than it was 60 years ago, but food banks are currently experiencing much greater demand than they used to. Those born into poor households can expect to live 9 years fewer than others, and the gap in life expectancy between rich and poor is increasing. Although, overall, men now follow the earlier trend among women in living longer than ever, for the first time since the late 19th century the difference in longevity between poor men and the more affluent is growing (Mayhew and Smith, 2016). Some necessary expenditures, such as housing, account for a greater proportion of household income than they did decades ago. Additionally, the poor are more likely than others to be victims of crime, and escaping poverty remains difficult. Upward social mobility has not increased for those born into poor households – there is about the same likelihood of their remaining poor as there was for their predecessors a century ago.

That the gap in longevity between poor and affluent men is now growing parallels a slightly older, and related, trend in inequality. After the 1970s, income and wealth inequality rose. With both, an earlier direction of change evident since the late Victorian era reversed. It might not be surprising, therefore, that inequality features more prominently in British political debate than just a few years ago. Indeed, since the world's financial crisis of 2008, public attention has increasingly been drawn to some aspects of this development. For instance, that the CEOs of FTSE 100 companies would earn more during the first three working days of 2018 than the typical British worker would in a year was well publicized. It was dubbed Fat Cat Thursday (Hodgson, 2018).

However, it is not only the poor, nor arguably mainly the poor, who have been vocal in their opposition to inegalitarian developments. Within a large sector of the middle class there has been a squeeze on certain aspects of their lives. One result is resentment at what is perceived by them as a worse situation than that faced previously by their older counterparts. Yet while their complaints may be directed primarily towards a generational inequality, it is their standing in relation to those with higher incomes and greater wealth in their *own* generation that is one cause of their situation. Like the poor, they are losing out to contemporaries who are more able to access key resources for which, largely, there is either a fixed or a limited supply. This point helps highlight two important features of poverty and inequality.

The first is that poverty and deprivation are relational conceptions, which is one valid point underpinning the assertion in Matthew's Gospel that "the poor are always with us". People are poor in relation to conditions in their own society. How the poor lived and survived 2000 years ago is not relevant to assessing the extent and impact of poverty in 21st century Britain. The British poor today are clearly much better off absolutely, but what matters is how effectively they can function and participate in contemporary society. What, if anything, can they do to improve their situations significantly without bearing absurdly high costs? Identifying poverty as being "relative" does not mean that there is necessarily deprivation in all contemporary societies, but it does mean that beyond a certain level of inequality there is poverty.

Deprivation is also *relational* in a separate way. Most poor people do not know just how wealthy the rich are, and, correspondingly, many of the latter believe that the poor must have higher spending power than they actually have. Some manual workers may know from the media that successful London barristers earn far more than they do, but quite how that affects the better-offs' lifestyles is largely unknown by those who are considerably less affluent. Much that barristers might buy – second homes in the country, expensive holidays or regular tickets to the opera – goes unobserved, and hence is only imperfectly imagined. We are more likely to perceive inequality by looking at those whose lives we know better – people who are more affluent than us, but not well beyond the range of our social acquaintances. What we are missing in relation to the latter can be seen by us, but it will usually give us a false impression of the money the best-off sections of the population really have. In other words, the groups to which people refer when making comparisons about wealth or income are restricted and are shaped mainly by imperfect personal knowledge. It has been known for at least 50 years that "comparative reference groups are limited in scope". There is always a gap between how unequal incomes are and how badly-off or well-off people believe themselves to be compared with others – the concept known by sociologists as "relative deprivation". There is a "considerable discrepancy between inequality and relative deprivation" (Runciman, 1966, p. 192).

A second feature of poverty and inequality is that those most disaffected by some aspects of social inequality, but in a position to protest effectively, are often not the least well-off. For example, one well-known interpretation of the origins of the French Revolution is that it was primarily elements in the bourgeoisie who facilitated it (Lefebvre, 1967). They had greater resources, including education, to promote dissent than the far more numerous poor. Any new or growing inequality adversely affecting relatively well-resourced groups has the potential to extend political conflict. It is not just declining living standards overall, or only small increases over time, that may act as a catalyst for their discontent. Today some sectors of the middle class have experienced much longer waits to enter the housing market, higher costs associated with attending university, and a reduction in the anticipated value of many occupational pensions. Since 2008 this experience has run in parallel with relatively low rates of growth in incomes and in the national economy. To a limited extent their new relative deprivation, by reference to their own social group at an earlier period, has helped to draw some public attention to broader issues of social inequality.

Why inequality arises and persists

Among many important questions relating to inequality are why it arises and how it persists. Various explanations have been proffered to account for the general phenomenon of inequality in many types of human society. Karl Marx's great contribution was to identify the role played by the means through which production was organized. For him, different modes of production generated different mechanisms that both created and then sustained inequality. His theory was that the capitalist mode of production had internal contradictions which eventually would result in vastly increased immiseration of the working class, such that the system would be overturned in a revolution. Irrespective of the many defects in his analysis, his key point is surely correct – that the emergence of capitalism in the 18th century fundamentally changed the mechanisms by which social inequality developed. Quite how it did so, however, has been the subject of considerable debate for over a century and a half.

A major limitation of Marx's arguments is that they largely ignore the role that other social divisions can play in capitalist societies, both independently of the means of production or in conjunction with it. Most especially, in many countries including Britain there are divisions based on gender and race that create inequalities. An obvious illustration of this: During the industrial era, access for the working class to the better paid and more interesting manual jobs was via apprenticeship systems. However, typically apprenticeships were open only to boys, so that, throughout their lives, most working-class women would be worse off than men because they either had to work in lower paid jobs or in an unpaid domestic role. The origins of this inequality were much older than capitalism. They lay in traditional cultural values about sex-based differences and in how different kinds of labour had been organized in peasant communities. Capitalist organization then modified how these divisions generated inequalities.

Thus, the significance of Marx's analysis cannot lie in its being comprehensive. Rather, it is primarily in his identification of the sheer scale and scope of the inequalities that necessarily arise within the class system. The social class into which you are born, and in which you work as an adult, is the major determinant of so many resources that you would need to lead the kind of life to which you might aspire. Typically, and even today, a girl from a middle-class family will acquire fewer such resources subsequently than will a middle-class boy, but usually both end up with more of these resources than either boys or girls from working class backgrounds. While class is not the end of any discussion about inequality in Britain, it is certainly the most obvious beginning. Curiously though, before the passage of the 2010 Equality Act, class background had not been included in British legislation, as had other groups at the sharp end of inequality – women, racial minorities and disabled people. Before the current decade it had not been one of "the responsibilities of the Minister for Women and Equality" (Harman, 2017, p. 292).

This century the most important and well-publicized contribution to answering the general question of "why does inequality arise?" has been that of Thomas Piketty (2014). His starting point is that, at the beginning of the capitalist era, societies were highly unequal and with no forces counteracting the concentration of wealth. However, when it was rapid, the facilitation of economic growth by capitalism would provide such a counterforce, and that would occur following major technological progress or from a large growth in population size. Alternatively, states could intervene to restrict the unequal distribution of wealth and income. In the absence of these factors, and under normal conditions, the push towards wealth being concentrated in the hands of a few would continue. Yet during the 20th century that momentum towards its concentration was interrupted by the consequences of two world wars and the intervening Great Depression. Those effects included the high rates of taxation required for conducting the wars, while the Depression created both bankruptcies and the subsequent development of welfare states. The holdings of the wealthy thereby declined. In addition, the Second World War was followed not just by state welfare provision in the advanced economies but also by more than a quarter of a century of relatively high economic growth. During those years the concentration of both income and wealth was reduced, with many advanced economies becoming more egalitarian than earlier. For Piketty, the successor to that era is one in which there have been few counterforces to the tendency towards greater inequality. Nevertheless, some analysts of inequality have argued that, irrespective of tendencies towards it, this is not an inevitable future (for example, Dorling, 2017).

While macro-analysis of this kind is crucial to understanding inequality, there are both significant differences between countries, as well as variations within them over time, in how inequality has been sustained. This diversity cannot be explained just by focussing on the macro-level of economic production, and it forms the context in which this short book is set. Its subject is the origins of contemporary inequality in Britain and of how the bases of inequality here have changed radically since the middle of the last century. Inequality is sustained by different factors now, some of which were the consequences of public policy, while others were the result of social and economic change. Moreover, any discussion must be wide-ranging in scope, because inequality relates not merely to the divergent levels of income or wealth people have. For example, the focus should also include the divergent treatment some people might receive in their social worlds, as well as to the prospects facing a person's descendants. Not all the relevant issues can be discussed in an extended way here, so that it is useful to commence this account by briefly introducing some of the key elements that are relevant when thinking about inequality, elements that then arise in various ways during later chapters.

Inequality of resources

Resources enable you to get what you want. Some highly specific resources are necessary for some wants. You cannot become a fighter pilot unless you have excellent eyesight. Being enfranchised is essential for voting in a democracy, although it is only a tiny individual resource and its impact depends on others voting too. Some resources are more general, in that they enable those who have them to obtain a wide range of the things that they want, need, or believe that they need. Especially in the most advanced economies, money is the most general of resources, one for which there is extensive data facilitating comparisons between countries. Usually, therefore, discussions of inequality begin with distributions of income and wealth. Of course, in understanding the functioning of some societies it may not necessarily be the best starting point. (India's caste system restricts someone's social opportunities there on the basis of the caste of their parents, so it is an obvious alternative for that country.) Certain forms of power are also quite general, although the range of their effectiveness in an advanced economy is typically less than with money.

The most widely used means of displaying income or wealth inequality is the Gini coefficient, a statistical measure of dispersion where full equality is recorded as 0 and complete inequality as 1. In Britain the coefficient for income rose dramatically during the 1980s. From the beginning of the 1960s it had fluctuated between 0.25 and 0.27, reaching a low value of 0.24 in 1979. Thereafter it rose to 0.4 in the early 1990s, then stabilized in the range of about 0.33–0.35. While a most effective illustration, the measure does not expose all that is relevant about income inequality. For example, at the very apex of personal earnings income inequality has increased significantly during the last 25 years. The share of all income in Britain received by the top 0.1 per cent of high earners rose from about 3 per cent of the total to just under 5 per cent, while overall growth in the share of total income was less among the rest of the top 5 or 10 per cent of earners (Tetlow, 2013).

Over time the greatest variation in share of income has also been that of the highest paid, rather than with any of the groups below them. In the late 1930s the top 10 per cent of earners took approximately 35 per cent of all income. By 1979 this had slowly reduced to 21 per cent of the total, but in the 1980s the trend reversed, and by 1990 their share was 27 per cent. By that decade the highest earning 20 per cent of the population accounted for about 43 per cent of all income, and that group has continued to receive between about 41 and 46 per cent this century (Lansley and Mack, 2013).

Today Britain's income inequality is amongst the highest in Europe, as well as being higher than Canada's though lower than that in the United States. By contrast, in 1979 Britain had a low measurement on the Gini index, comparable today only to that of Norway. Britain's rush to income inequality started earlier than in most countries, and even by the mid-1980s the policies of the Thatcher government had propelled it to being one of the most inegalitarian countries in Europe. Others' trajectories towards less equality started later, so that, *proportionately*, in the period between the mid-1980s and 2014 the rate at which they were becoming less egalitarian was greater than the United Kingdom's. Yet, in the unequal income stakes Britain continues to lag well behind the European average (Table 1.1).

Measuring wealth inequality is subject to greater complexity and more disagreement than is usual for income (Alvaredo, Atkinson, and Morelli, 2016). One important issue is what to include as part of someone's capital and, in some cases, how to calculate its monetary value. Nonetheless, in comparative perspective, the data that is available tends to indicate a rather different pattern of concentration for Britain than with income. Wealth inequality is close to the average for OECD countries, being lower than in Germany or the Netherlands, and much lower than in the United States. Furthermore, Norway, with income distribution that is now far more equal than Britain's, has similar inequality in the distribution of wealth (Table 1.2) (OECD, 2017, p. 10). Nevertheless, to a high degree, capital in Britain remains unequally distributed, and possession of those forms of capital that are most easily converted into money directly affects the life chances of someone's descendants. Not only might they inherit much of that capital but its conversion into money earlier facilitates the enhancing of their opportunities whilst they are young.

Obviously, possessing a range of generalized resources, including money and power, increases the ways in which you can try to get what you want. Nevertheless, with some resources how much you can get of the things you want, or how easily you can get them, depends on how much of the relevant resources you have

TABLE 1.1 Gini coefficients of disposable income inequality in OECD member countries for 2014 (or latest year) and for mid-1980s (when available)

	2014, or Nearest year	*Mid-1980s*
Denmark	0.25	0.22
Slovenia	0.26	
Finland	0.26	0.21
Czech Republic	0.26	0.23
Belgium	0.27	0.28
Slovak Republic	0.27	
Austria	0.28	
Sweden	0.28	
Luxembourg	0.28	0.25
Netherlands	0.28	0.27
Hungary	0.29	0.27
Germany	0.29	0.25
France	0.29	0.30
Poland	0.30	
Ireland	0.31	
Italy	0.32	
Portugal	0.34	
Greece	0.34	0.35
Spain	0.34	
Latvia	0.35	
United Kingdom	**0.36**	**0.33**
Estonia	0.36	
Average for OECD members in European Union	**0.29**	**0.26**
Iceland	0.29	
Norway	0.25	0.23
Canada	0.32	0.29
Japan	0.33	0.30
United States	0.38	0.34
Average for All OECD members	**0.32**	**0.29**

Source: OECD (2017, p. 8).

relative to those held by others. This is the point of the ancient aphorism that "in the land of the blind the one-eyed man is king". There this specific resource gives him a huge advantage currently, but its value declines when another sighted person appears, and it continues to diminish further as the sighted population increases. Often, though, having a large holding in one resource can compensate for paucity in another, though it does not do so always, and indeed sometimes the latter can weaken the advantage given by the former. However, as noted at the outset here, social inequality in modern societies is usually cumulative, and rarely is it just money that the poor lack.

TABLE 1.2 Share of wealth owned by top 10 per cent of population (as percentage of total wealth) – for selected European and other countries

Austria	60
Netherlands	56
Germany	56
Portugal	52
Luxembourg	50
France	49
United Kingdom	**47**
Finland	46
Italy	45
Belgium	45
Norway	45
Spain	43
Greece	39
Slovak Republic	33
United States	75
OECD Average	**48**

Source: OECD (2017, p. 10).

Britain's social inequality emanates mainly from social class, but until the later 20th century the main "engine" maintaining class divisions was not so much income as status, which itself derived primarily from whether your job was manual (or not), breeding, and lifestyle. Status was valuable in itself but, additionally, was a resource enabling a person to protect other means that made their lifestyle possible. Until the 1950s that status hierarchy was exclusively a white one, partly because until then the nonwhite population was so small. During the Second World War, its very size had contributed to a largely negative public reaction to the hostile attitudes of white American service personnel to their fellow African-Americans. After 1947, migration from its collapsing Empire, and especially from the Caribbean and South Asia, resulted in more complex reactions to race in Britain. However, for the most part, those who viewed race in hierarchical terms did not link it to the older (white) status hierarchy. It was understood as a separate line of social division.

The relative demise of social status as the mainspring of social inequality within the white population was arguably the most significant change in British society after about 1970. In its place, money became the dominant vehicle for preserving inequality. While possessing little intrinsic value, it is a truly flexible resource that can be put to many purposes. That flexibility facilitates more intense competition with others to get what you want – whether that be access for your children to institutions providing the best and most prestigious educational credentials, or, perhaps, sought-after tickets to rock concerts or theatrical productions. Gone was a world in which educational credentials mattered little, and private schooling was largely a holding camp for middle- and upper-class children until they were old enough to have an occupation. Gone too were social arrangements where someone might need an invitation, via personal contacts, to the more desirable social events and entertainments. In the new regime, status was much less of a barrier to entry by the poor, but lack of money certainly was. Perhaps the most important feature of money, though, is how it can facilitate doing well in positional competition – that is, improving your own position within some hierarchical structure at the expense of others.

For many of the better paid positions in contemporary Britain the most significant of these structures are linked to educational credentials. What matters now is not a credential demonstrating your proficiency but one that can be used to indicate that you are *more proficient* than your competitors for a scholarship, job, or whatever. Alongside the relative rise of money within the British class system, are structures where hiring (and promoting) the supposed "best" trumps hiring the "proficient" (however rigorously "proficiency" is defined). The crucial problem with this is that the means of determining who, of the proficient, will be the "best" at any activity are necessarily extremely limited. Yet ours is a society in which it has become a central organizing principle. It underpins the widely accepted notion that higher pay is justifiable on grounds of merit – that is, we should pay the supposedly most meritorious (the "best") more than anyone else.

That notion is sophistry whose ascendancy in political debate is illuminated by a change in the English language. The word *meritocracy* was first coined in the mid-20th century by sociologist Michael Young (1958) in his much-publicized satirical novel, *The Rise of the Meritocracy*. He used the term to denote the elite in a new kind of dystopia, one that would eventually be overthrown by popular opposition in 2033. This elite had skills, but their deployment mainly benefitted the members of the elite itself. In later decades, though, the words *meritocracy* and *meritocratic* were used very differently – to denote social arrangements that are superior because people with the supposedly greatest merit occupy senior positions. Unfortunately, as will become clearer later, the information on which anyone might predict successfully who will turn out to be the "best" for any given position is so limited that the link between actual *relative* merit and relative rewards is weak. Moreover, the assertion that sheer merit underpins meritocracy helps to perpetuate existing inequalities (Littler, 2017). As Young had imagined, British society has moved from one kind of privileged elite to another, without the latter's justification to forming that new elite being much stronger than those of its predecessor, where it was social origins that mattered.

Inequality of opportunities

Social mobility is a complex phenomenon (Lawler and Payne, 2018). When asked if they approve of it, most people typically respond that they do. The idea that those who have little should be able to improve their income, the kind of job they have, and so on, is appealing. But what of downward mobility? Presumably, if it were caused by profligacy, extreme idleness or excessive risk-taking, then it too might well command considerable support. In Victorian Britain, attitudes to mobility downwards were mixed. Certainly, those experiencing it for these reasons commanded little sympathy. Yet it was also widely feared at the time, both because it was relatively common and was frequently the result of unforeseeable circumstances, such as the early death of a family's main breadwinner. Today little attention is paid to the downwardly mobile, except most recently with respect to the rise of homelessness.

What many seem to want are opportunities for upward mobility but with only limited downward movement. Indeed, today talking about social mobility usually implies a reference to the former while ignoring the latter. For a large part of the 20th century this win-win outcome, or "having your cake and eating it", was partly evident in Britain. The era of the working class would come, but then go (Todd, 2014). The proportion of white-collar, middle-class, occupations increased and that of manual, working-class, jobs declined. Furthermore, lower mortality rates, and after 1945 state provision, eased the worst aspects of social deprivation, greatly reducing both the incidence of the Victorian nightmare and the severity of its consequences.

The modest upward social mobility that there was during the last century, facilitated primarily by changes in the labour market, helped dampen objections and protests to various aspects of inequality in Britain. Some people, whose parents, grandparents, or great-grand parents had been working class, now held middle-class jobs. Yet, if you have been born working class within the last 20 years, the likelihood is that those three generations of your ancestors were of the same class as yourself. Absent the labour market shift away from manual labour, then upward social mobility is no greater now than a century ago. Leaving aside that transformation, the main, though limited, vehicle for exiting the working class for much of the last century had been via education. Working-class children, who from 1907 acquired scholarships to grammar schools (and later those who after 1944 passed the 11+ examination), would be taught the academic skills required for white-collar employment. (For girls, this opened up opportunities to become secretaries but few higher-level jobs, with marriage further blighting their prospects for continuing employment or advancement.) Most of their social class peers did not acquire these skills, and certainly did not possess the important status symbol of having attended a grammar school.

On leaving those schools and entering the labour market, this relatively small minority of working-class boys were then only in limited competition with their middle-class grammar school contemporaries or with those who had attended private schools. Schooling gave middle-class children the minimum skills necessary, but it was social contacts that usually helped them into their jobs. That system would change in the second half of the 20th century, and with it would be introduced a radically different means by which equality of opportunity would be restricted. The educational credentials that a child had acquired – both the level they had reached, and the relative quality of the credential awarded – came to matter much more. Irrespective of class, opportunities to obtain the best jobs required children to be drawn into competition with each other: to get the highest grades at secondary school, to be admitted to the most prestigious universities based on those grades, to obtain the best class of degree, and, increasingly, later to obtain postgraduate qualifications.

Relatively, in this new world, high intelligence plays a reduced role for the working-class child, because available financial resources matter too. At all stages having money enhances the value of intelligence and hard work. Families who have it can pay for educationally superior private schools, extra-school private tuition, or to relocate to the catchment areas of the "best" state schools. The hopes of those who had supported the switch to comprehensive schools in the 1960s and 1970s, because supposedly this would facilitate more equal opportunities, were largely dashed. One of the main reasons for this was a failure to understand that geography mattered. (Typically, different social classes were already occupying different territories, with middle-class areas often having superior state schools in theirs; that tendency would be reinforced after comprehensivization.) Again, for a greatly rising number of university graduates, the anticipated positive effect on their incomes was not realized. It is, perhaps, ironic that the one vehicle that had facilitated a small amount of upward social mobility previously now formed the main barrier to it.

Inequality between whom?

Who are the relevant people to consider when examining and discussing inequality between individuals? The obvious answer for this book is people in Britain, but does this mean all its citizens, all its resident, or what? Moreover, to be some kind of egalitarian, does this mean that you must be taking account of everyone within the country? To be a thorough-going egalitarian most certainly. However, in several countries there have been political movements with overtly egalitarian aims that have excluded some groups from consideration because they are simply regarded as not possessing full membership of the "people". In contrast to this are claims for greater inclusion beyond those currently alive in Britain – for those yet to be born – that they should be treated as the equals of those living now.

To take the exclusion issue first. Historically some populist movements have been of this kind. Even though today populism is often regarded as being merely an aggressive element of the political Right, and hence anti-egalitarian, some populists combined vigorously egalitarian policies with discrimination against particular groups. For instance, the American populist movement of the 1880s had clear egalitarian aims, especially in its early years, though from the 1890s its leaders in the South often linked this to support for racial segregation. Even as late as the 1970s there remained nationally influential Southern politicians who still pursued equality but had a much-restricted view as to who should be considered full members of American society. In Congress from 1928 to 1976, Wright Patman was a prime exemplar of this. Upon the Texan's death, the *New York Times* wrote of him:

> To Wright Patman, the root of all evil was the concentration of economic power in the hands of a small number of bankers, business executives and government officials. He spent his life trying to expose the evils and restrict the power, and his record contained many successes and many failures (8 March 1976).

Yet in 1956 Patman had also been one of the best-known signatories to the Southern Manifesto, a public statement of opposition by Southern politicians to racial integration in schools ordered by the US Supreme Court 3 years earlier, a decision that had reversed legally based racial segregation in the United States.

Including those yet to be born as part of "the people", when doing so could affect adversely the welfare of those living, is a consideration only for those societies that have moved beyond subsistence. At higher economic levels, valuing the future – other than as an aspect of religious practice – becomes feasible. The Victorians started to make major investments in expensive capital projects, such as sewers, that would alleviate the adverse conditions of urbanization for their generation, but with much of the benefit to be enjoyed by future Britons. However, it was not until the rise of concerns about environmental changes in the 1970s that there was extensive debate about the desirability of policies designed to protect the interests of subsequent generations, when that protection would usually impose costs or restrictions on the living. Previously, outside academic analyses, the issue of unequal provision for different generations was little discussed. One reason was that, in the aggregate, successive British generations were better off than their predecessors, and although unequally distributed, the benefits were not confined exclusively to the few. Long-term economic growth since industrialization, combined with slowly decreasing inequalities in wealth and income, made this possible for about the first three quarters of the 20th century. Although periodic recessions and depressions had interrupted these long-term trends, typically those born 25 years later than their immediate predecessors would be materially better off than them. The future was protected.

During the present century, however, there has been growing controversy over whether so-called Millennials, who are usually understood as those born between about 1982 and 2004, have in some ways experienced worse conditions than the previous generation. Although it is not always stated openly, many proponents of this line of argument imply that the Millennials have been treated unequally, and that their successors might well be too (for example, Willetts, 2010).

At first glance this aspect of political debate might appear puzzling. Between 1980 and 2014, the British gross domestic product (GDP) rose at an average rate of 2.2 per cent per year. The occasions on which GDP declined were few, although there was an unusually large fall (of over 4 per cent) in 2009. Most Millennials had far more capacity for buying goods and services than any of their predecessors, and, because of technological innovations since 1980, they were superior in most ways to those available only a few years earlier. Thus, it might be argued that, like their predecessors, their futures had been protected. However, compared with their immediate predecessors, many Millennials are in a worse position in the housing market, will have lower private pensions, and have paid more for their higher education. Moreover, some financial organizations have predicted that the lower rates of growth in the world economy evident since the financial crisis of 2008 could continue for years (KPMG, 2018). Thus, the public discontent exhibited in recent years by those who believe that they are experiencing a worse deal than earlier generations might be expected to persist.

Yet it is the poor who are always the worst to suffer in hard times. Most have to rent their accommodations, which now accounts for about one-third of their net incomes, given a national housing shortage. Additionally, their chances of being upwardly mobile are no greater than they were a century ago for their predecessors, partly because the system of educational credentials is geared towards the better off (Goldthorpe, 2016). Many poor pensioners have a tiny occupational pension, if any at all, with which to supplement a state pension, and so on.

Consequently, while Matthew's Gospel might be correct in its assertion that "the poor are always with us", neo-Marxists may not have been quite so accurate in believing that it is the impoverishment of the working class that is the main springboard for social discontent. In the vanguard of those arguing that they are worse off, by comparison with those older than themselves, are social groups whose expectations have been reduced in a country that is wealthier than it has ever been. Moreover, these are groups that have more of the political resources that the poor generally lack, to protest and debate their relative impoverishment effectively. Arguably, they are one of the main causes of inequality returning to the forefront of political debate in the 21st century.

Different dimensions of inequality

Just as the question "Inequality between whom?" has to be raised when discussing inequality, so too must the parallel question "Inequality with respect to what?". Answering the one usually involves trying to answer the other. Social class is not the only reason why some individuals and social groups lack the opportunities that others have. For at least part of their lives, many women are unable to take full advantage of opportunities that might otherwise be available because of the role that they play in performing the unpaid labour of domestic work or as carers – for their children, and for elderly or disabled relatives. Because this labour falls outside any market system, eliminating the inequality generated would require different forms of state intervention than those used to reduce inequalities originating in class differences. Thus, the idea of a basic income, one to be paid by the state to all adults, is seen by its advocates as one means of correcting this kind of inegalitarian bias in market economies (for example, as by Van Parijs, 1995, and McKay, 2005).

In addition, opportunities for some have been, and continue to be, denied either on an individual basis or because of discrimination against one of the social groups to which they belong. While some of this may be overt prejudice, it can be just as virulent in creating forms of inequality when it is covert or is the product of systems that, in their effects though not intentionally, work against the interests of some groups.

At the beginning of the 20th century there were still some laws that discriminated directly against particular social groups. Thus, the practice of male homosexuality was illegal, though lesbianism never had been. Women could not vote, and younger women remained unfranchised until 1928. However, most discrimination against individual members of specific groups was neither sanctioned nor prohibited by law. More common than legally sanctioned discrimination was denial of equal treatment for one of two reasons.

One lay within institutions of government and law where corruption, personal contacts, incompetence, personal prejudice and so on could deny a person equal treatment, depending on who they were. Mostly this occurred, as it still does, before the formal stages of applying a law or regulation began. It is easier at that stage for action or inaction to remain beyond public view, and hence remain hidden, unpublicized, or ignored. How open a state institution is to supervision or scrutiny is one factor affecting how much equality under the law there can be. For decades during the 20th century it was widely known that some sections of the Metropolitan Police were highly corrupt, but the organization's virtual autonomy long prevented or delayed extensive effective reform. As the Conservative minister Ken Clarke was later to say of that autonomy when he became Home Secretary in 1992:

> ... for some peculiar reason the Home Secretary was... personally responsible for the Metropolitan Police, acting as its police authority. I soon realized, however, that I was as powerless as the county councillors and magistrates who made up the largely useless local police authorities across the country
> *(Clarke, 2016, pp. 281–282).*

Inside private organizations the opportunities to discriminate were even greater, with inequality being perpetuated through widespread, but unspoken, beliefs, values, and assumptions that determined the behaviour of those who could exclude or harm others. Thus, for most of the 20th century, Catholics in Northern Ireland could not obtain jobs in shipyards there, women were frequently paid less than men for equivalent jobs, and racial minorities could be refused the rental of a flat. Much of the egalitarian effort in the later decades of the last century was directed towards reforms that could provide some safeguards against this kind of behaviour. In part, it entailed enshrining in law certain kinds of rights for individuals who were members of a specified group. Yet, as important as these rights themselves was their role in stimulating other informal strategies for transforming attitudes and behaviour towards those groups.

During the later 20th century, social diversity in Britain became both more widely recognized and accepted. Conformity to the values and behaviour of hierarchies, in which white, heterosexual men were supposed to be the natural occupants of their apex, was eroding. Some of the inequalities these hierarchies had fostered were subject to challenge, though not necessarily overthrown. However, this empowerment of the individual, through reducing inequality, did not always have beneficial consequences. In the political arena it could make more difficult the reconciling of different interests and opinions within British society. Especially with the advent of social media, the reconciliation of differences had to be undertaken under conditions in which opinions could more easily be expressed aggressively and with intimidation. The internet made it possible for anyone to exhibit troll-like behaviour, whereas in a face-to-face world physical appearance and demeanour often matters in establishing the plausibility of a threat. Along with other factors, this new kind of equality facilitated more frequent and overt conflict in the public arena between different values and opinions. At the same time, everyone having the capability of being heard via the internet tended to weaken the attention paid to those who had expertise on various matters. The latter's ability to provide evidence in support of opinions now counted for less in a world in which anyone could get an opinion aired. One individual's opinion was as good as another's, something that made both social management and government more complex, and especially in democracies.

The dimensions of social, economic, and political life in which people want greater equality alter over time. In this regard, during the early decades of the present century Britain is far removed from the place that it was during the 1960s and the immediately preceding decades. This is not an expression of nostalgia or sentimentality by the author but an evaluation of the scale of change over more than half a century. As L. P. Hartley observed in 1953 in his novel *The Go-Between*, "The past is a foreign country: they do things differently there." When examining inequality in Britain today, it is necessary to understand how we arrived at the present from that foreign country.

References

Alvaredo, Facundo, Atkinson, Anthony B., and Morelli, Salvatore (2016). "The Challenge of Measuring UK Wealth Inequality in the 2000s", *Fiscal Studies*, 37(1), pp. 13–33.

Clarke, Ken (2016). *Kind of Blue: A Political Memoir*. London: Macmillan.

Dorling, Danny (2017). *Do We Need Economic Inequality?* Cambridge: Polity Press.

Goldthorpe, John H. (2016). "Social Mobility in Modern Britain: Changing Structure, Constant Process", *Journal of the British Academy*, 4, pp. 89–111.

Harman, Harriet (2017). *A Woman's Work*. London: Allen Lane.

Hodgson, Camilla (2018). "Fat Cat Thursday: FTSE 100 CEOs Will Earn More in 3 Days Than Workers' Annual Salary", *Business Insider*, 4 January.

KPMG (2018). *Moderate, Occasionally Rough. Visibility Poor: UK Economic Outlook*. London: KPMG.

Lansley, Stewart and Mack, Joanna (2013). "A More Unequal Country?", *Poverty and Social Exclusion*, 16 April.

Lawler, Steph and Payne, Geoff (eds.) (2018). *Social Mobility for the 21st Century: Everyone a Winner?* London: Routledge.

Lefebvre, Georges (1967). *The Coming of the French Revolution*. Princeton, NJ: Princeton University Press.

Littler, Jo (2017). *Against Meritocracy: Culture, Power and Myths of Mobility*. London: Routledge.

Mayhew, Les and Smith, David (2016). *An Investigation into Inequalities in Adult Lifespan.* London: Cass Business School, City University.

McKay, Alisa (2005). *The Future of Social Security Policy: Women, Work and a Citizen's Basic Income.* London: Routledge.

OECD Centre for Opportunity and Equality (2017). *Understanding the Socio-Economic Divide in Europe.* Paris: OECD.

Piketty, Thomas (2014). *Capital in the Twenty-First Century.* Cambridge, MA: Belknap Press.

Runciman, W. G. (1966). *Relative Deprivation and Social Justice: A Study of Social Attitudes to Social Inequality in Twentieth-Century Britain.* London: Routledge and Kegan Paul.

Tetlow, Gemma (2013). "Is Income Inequality Increasing in the UK?", *Financial Times*, 16 April.

Todd, Selina (2014). *The People: The Rise and Fall of the Working Class, 1910–2010.* London: John Murray.

Van Parijs, Philippe (1995). *Real Freedom for All, What (If Anything) Can Justify Capitalism?* Oxford: Clarendon Press.

Willetts, David (2010). *The Pinch: How the Baby Boomers Took Their Children's Future – And Why They Should Give It Back.* London: Atlantic Books.

Young, Michael (1958). *The Rise of the Meritocracy.* Harmondsworth: Penguin.

2

MONEY AND STATUS

Although money is the most generalized of social resources, allowing us to obtain many of the things we want, not everything can be bought. As the Beatles once sang, "money can't buy me love". It cannot because, as with friendship, love is one of those things that is dissolved or transformed into something else by the act of buying (Sandel, 2012, p. 94). However, with varying degrees of complexity and delay, many resources – houses, stocks and shares, and so on – are convertible into money, and can be spent or handed on to the next generation of one's family. The potential for converting these resources into money, when combined with the social practice of children inheriting from their parents, has a major impact on long-term inequality. Typically, wealthy families are resource rich not just for one generation, but often for many in succession. Fiona Devine makes the point more formally, about one aspect of the intergenerational effects of money. In her study of how parents help their children get good jobs, she notes one key feature of money's flexibility. Financial resources are

> the most important resource because they are exclusive goods (not owned by others) that can be easily transmitted … in comparison to cultural and social resources that are inclusive goods (which can be owned by others) that are less easily transmitted
>
> *(Devine, 2004, p. 5).*

It might be expected, therefore, that the shift to a less egalitarian distribution of money since 1979 would be at the centre of political conflict. However, the Labour Party's response has generally remained muted, partly because of the declining relative size of the working class. For the Right, overt opposition to greater equality can pose electoral risks, and in countering various policy proposals announced by those on the Left, Right-wing politicians and journalists often couch their opposition obliquely. Much favoured anti-egalitarian terms are the "politics of envy" and "social engineering". Frequently both are invoked against egalitarian proposals in ways that not only bypass the issues at hand but, in most cases, lack content, although not some emotive power; it is more akin to what Americans call raising a Bronx Cheer.[1] The use of the phrase "politics of envy" is indeed curious, since there are two obvious reasons why an attempt by the Left to mobilize on the basis of envy would usually be wholly unsuccessful as a political strategy.

Envy, inequality and financial power

One reason is that knowledge about the financial resources available to social groups other than one's own is limited, a point introduced in Chapter 1. The deprived have little sense of just how well off the affluent really are, nor indeed how many of them there are. In contemporary societies, with considerable physical separation of the deprived from the affluent, the former's experiences tend to depress the extent of perceived inequality and to diminish the potential for mobilizing against financial inequality.

A second reason is that only rarely is resentment about income or wealth inequality driven by the spending opportunities open to the rich. It is propelled by either how some of the rich obtain their money or the adverse consequences of its uses. Even a committed egalitarian may not find it unjust or perverse that a star footballer who is their favourite player, or a rock star whose music they like, earns many times more than they do. The income of stars derives indirectly from that person and from many others being willing to pay to see them perform. This observation is scarcely new. It was a famous argument used in support of a minimal state by the philosopher Robert Nozick (1974). He cited people's willingness to pay extra to see basketball games featuring the star player Wilt Chamberlain, as a way of demonstrating his claim that attempts to justify fixed distributions of wealth in a society were unjust. Nozick was tapping into the basic idea that, when there seems to be a direct link between inequality and what we would willingly pay for, a plausible case for equality is weakened.

Controversy about the income sources of the rich typically arises when evasion of moral or legal responsibilities is involved, especially when it is at the expense of others. Although the notion of "paying one's fair share of taxes" is necessarily vague, the idea has played an important part in public evaluations of the remuneration of high earners when, for whatever reason, they come to be widely known. Individual judgements might be inconsistent, and sometimes wrong, but they derive from essentially moral considerations, and not envy.

Opposition to those who are richer also develops when it is widely believed that their use of the wealth will have adverse consequences for others. At one extreme is the possible link between inequality and the capacity it can provide the rich in exercising power directly over others. The classic, and extreme, example of this is the company town where the single employer's financial resources create an overwhelming, and unfair, advantage in any labour disputes. More commonly, the fear of the "power of money" is that expenditures by the wealthier will distort the ability of the less rich to get what they want or need. Thus, for several decades from about the 1960s the Left saw private health care provision as having a negative impact on the National Health Service (NHS) and for the equality of provision that underpinned the NHS. Opposition to it centred on NHS facilities being used for private treatment by hospital consultants contracted to the NHS, but who were undertaking private work as well. It was believed that this practice would result ultimately in fewer potential resources being available to non-private patients. The market, which was accessible only by the more affluent, would squeeze the NHS's ability to deliver its services – to the detriment of the worse off.

Later this particular issue was transformed, thereby becoming less controversial. The role of private sector provision did expand, but not directly at the expense of NHS provision. Expansion enabled private treatment to be concentrated in non-NHS units, partly reducing the perception of direct competition for physical facilities. Moreover, while the market could often offer faster consultations and treatments, as well as more pleasant hospital experiences, usually its treatments were for less essential procedures. In part, further growth in that health sector was constrained by the much higher premiums that insurance companies would have had to charge, were they to offer alternatives to most of the NHS's core services. Private health care became not so much a competitor to the NHS, as a complement to it – at least for the wealthier. The issue of inequality *per se* would remain sidelined from the later 20th century as the focus of attention on the NHS changed – first, to the adverse impact of creating internal markets within it and then to its overall underfunding.

Another example of market conditions changing, thereby altering public perceptions of a potentially new inequality, arose with the expansion of cable television in the early 1990s. While the conceivable social impact of this development would be much less than in the NHS, it raised similar concerns about equality of access to a service.

To increase its subscriptions, Sky TV began offering lucrative contracts to major sports for exclusive live coverage. At the outset, it was assumed that only those with higher incomes could afford to view major sporting events on Sky, including ones previously on terrestrial television. Subscriptions would be beyond the financial reach of many of the less well off, thereby depriving them of access. The Conservative government's response was to designate some events – the FA Cup Final and cricket's Test matches included – as being of major national importance. They should be accessible to all, and thus could be broadcast only on terrestrial channels. Within just a few years, however, as the purchase of cable television subscriptions increased massively, the list of these protected events shrank. Undoubtedly the political influence of the Murdoch media empire, Sky TV's owners, helped facilitate the change, but the strength of the argument from inequality had unquestionably become weaker. Like share values, inequalities can fall as well as rise.

Money, status and social class

Although money has always been essential in understanding social inequality, how it creates and preserves them has shifted since the second half of the 20th century. At the heart of this change lies a major mutation in the British class system, which has altered both how inequality is maintained and the nature of division within the political system.

For decades after the 1920s Britain had two-party politics reflecting a class divide, although the basis of social inequality was never that easy to comprehend. Essentially, the class system consisted of two separate but inter-connected structures. One was an *economic* "hierarchy" – based on inequalities in income and wealth. The other was founded on *esteem and prestige* – a social hierarchy in which it was relative position that counted. The link between the two was occupation, and the type of occupation was the major determinant of social class. Usually the kind of job a person had, and in the case of heterosexual couples that meant primarily the man's occupation, was a good indicator of their income. While recognizing that someone had a similar level of income as yours could suggest that they were a social equal, there were important exceptions (Runciman, 1966, p. 38).[2] This was one of the main reasons why each of the two largest classes – leaving aside the tiny, though rich and politically influential, aristocracy – was itself divided. Other members of the same class often did not identify fully with those considered "inferior" within their own class.

The working class constituted nearly three-quarters of the total population as late as 1951 (McKibbin, 1998, p. 160). Within it differences between skilled and unskilled workers, and the partly related divide between "respectable" and "not respectable" members of the class, mattered to many.[3] Moreover, how significant being working class was as a source of personal identity varied greatly between individuals. The strongest identifiers tended to be men from families with a trade union member, who were employed in a large firm, and lived in a major urban area. The fewer of these characteristics within the family, the less being working class drove their political beliefs and influenced how they understood the options open to them, and their children, in leading their lives. That the working class was not unified was one of several reasons that it was difficult for the Labour Party ever to muster more than two-thirds of that class's voters behind it. The middle class acted more cohesively in politics; given their minority status its members had to when defending their own interests, but there were still fissures within it. That would change slowly in the mid-20th century, by which time this class was growing rapidly and, more significantly, diversifying in character.

Typically, clerks, whose numbers were among those in decline, had been proud of their not being working class. Nevertheless, they were looked down on by much of the rest of the middle class because their tastes and cultural values were regarded as inferior. Throughout the class such snobbery did not derive primarily from comparative income. Families in which the husband had a recognized profession could regard people "in trade" as being inferior, irrespective of how successful or "respectable" the latter's businesses were.

Yet, for all the divisions within both social classes, the primary split between the working and the middle class really mattered. There were clear barriers between the two that both sides recognized. Sometimes physical barriers were constructed to reinforce separation. Among the most notorious were the two Cutteslowe Walls, erected in North Oxford in 1934, to prevent the mainly working-class residents of a neighbouring council estate from being able to enter directly a private housing development. They were finally demolished in 1959. (Unlike the walled and gated "communities" of more recent times, which are more common in the United States than the United Kingdom, the walls cut off existing public roads to prevent easy access, and were not the construction of a quasi-fortress.)

Women who married "below" their own social class were less likely than men who did so to pass on their original status to their children. Because, outside of wartime conditions, women faced major barriers to entering most white-collar careers, let alone progressing in them, their own class background usually counted for less to the fortunes of their children than the occupation of the father. For men who "married down", the direct long-term impact on their children's prospects was smaller.

Moving downwards into the working class had many causes but there was just one main route upwards, and that was via education. However, all but a small minority of working-class children failed the scholarship examinations or their successor, the 11+. Places were rationed, the establishment of new grammar schools was slow, and thus passing the 11+ was most certainly not about a child meeting a fixed, pre-determined, educational standard. No more than about 20 per cent of all secondary school children were ever admitted to grammar schools, and most of the pupils were middle class. At first, it was merely attending one for a few years that mattered to those anxious working-class parents concerned that their children not enter manual jobs later. Especially from the early 1960s, educational *credentials*, obtained in schools and universities, would come to acquire their own high status. Although an element of the status system earlier, for many they were much less important then, yet their value not only survived but became greatly enhanced. Thus the status of being a graduate would continue to matter subsequently, even when for many it was not accompanied by high financial rewards. Today being admitted to university is still esteemed, even though throughout the present century about one-third of all graduates have been working in non-graduate occupations 5 years after completing their degrees (Office of National Statistics, 2013, p. 14).[4]

For at least half of the 20th century, most middle-class adolescents did not have to pursue educational credentials to the highest level. Once they had the academic skills necessary for various kinds of employment, family connections were the usual route to obtaining a job. Consequently, to succeed in obtaining a non-manual job, the working-class child typically needed to achieve more, and indeed those in grammar schools usually stayed there for longer than their middle-class counterparts (Spens Report, 1938, p. 97).[5]

Cultural factors reinforced class differences based on occupation – speech, accents, dress, and so on; all tended to generate stereotypes of how people in different classes should behave. (This was famously satirized in a television sketch, "The Frost Report on Class", in 1966.) Furthermore, despite well-known examples of movement across the class divide, overall it was uncommon. Obviously, most members of the middle class were horrified at the thought that their children might "descend" into the working class, or that their own social position might be threatened by being classified (by others) with those whom they regarded as inferiors. Among the working class were some who were proud of that class and had no ambitions to "advance" above it. Yet many did aspire to middle-class status, or at least to the opportunities and privileges associated with it.

Location mattered. "The geographical separation of the classes had ... its origins in the nineteenth century and was a remorseless process" (McKibbin, 1998, p. 101). Late 19th century urbanization had seen the proliferation of large areas of new "villas", such as in Birmingham's Edgbaston, into which the middle class were increasingly concentrated. Yet territorial ghettoization of the two classes was never complete. Poorly paid clerks might have little choice but to live in the same street as better paid manual workers.

The sub-class of domestic servants straddled the class divide, but in a particular way. Pay was low and their work was certainly manual. However, many were supposed by employers to imbibe some of their own attributes, especially speech, through living and working in their houses. Live-in employees often "enjoyed" poor accommodation but in prime locations.[6] To the extent that it succeeded, domestic service tended to reinforce greater social and political conservatism, especially among women because they were employed disproportionately in this non-unionized workforce.

In the largest cities older patterns of residence still persisted, especially in London. Apart from districts in the expanding East End, a relatively short walk could often take a manual worker from home into a neighbourhood that was uniformly middle class. In general, though, increased physical separation of the classes was becoming evident. This, and the demise of domestic service, helped further reduce popular knowledge of "how the other half lived". For their part, only a minority of the "educated classes" ever read the growing number of publications and studies showing just how poor the poor really were, and how many of them there were.

Geographical separation of the classes is a proverbial double-edged sword, although with one edge distinctly sharper than the other. Concentrations of the working class in larger, urban, areas helped solidify their class identity initially, an important catalyst in political mobilization. However, separation also reinforced various aspects of inequality, and some of its effects persist. For obvious reasons, those who commit crimes are more likely to do so in or near their own communities, making the poor especially vulnerable to others who are also deprived in various ways. Again, families who move to new accommodation in the catchment areas of superior schools can further weaken the schools that their children leave. In deprived areas the bases for local taxation are lower. Of course, some aspects of separation mattered less as higher national standards improved conditions throughout the country. For example, over decades infant mortality has continued to decline generally. Nevertheless, there remain significant differences in its incidence between poor and wealthier local authorities (Norman, Gregory, Dorling, and Baker, 2008). Overall, because of both cultural factors and fewer opportunities, living in deprived areas with other poor people typically reinforces the effects of being poor oneself.

Transformation of the class system

While the class divide persists in Britain, since the middle of the past century the relationship between the two hierarchies constituting it has been transformed. From 1980, of course, the economic "hierarchy" became more elongated, with greater inequality of income and wealth developing. Commencing even earlier, though, inequalities in esteem tended to weaken and are now less significant in marking the basic divide. Who your parents and grandparents were came to matter less than the financial resources they could either spend on your behalf or that you could inherit on their deaths. While not wholly irrelevant, accent and cultural factors make entry into middle-class careers less difficult for working-class adolescents. (Outside labour markets, the "cultural" pillar of the British class structure did not collapse completely, and social snobbery persisted.[7]) More importantly, the demise of family and other connections in getting a job, and the corresponding rise of supposed expertise, has facilitated this development. A written reference for an applicant by someone unknown to you used to entail more risk than the word of a friend or close acquaintance: you had less reason to trust them, especially when you would expect to have no further links to them. Where systems of trust do survive, however, personal contacts can still play an important role in access, even for junior posts. Thus, Devine's study in the 1990s demonstrated how significant contacts were in starting medical careers in Britain. Those taught by the senior staff at the leading teaching hospitals (in London and Manchester) would have mentors who were important in providing access to consultancy posts in hospitals, and who also had some contacts for positions in general practice (Devine, 2004, p. 122).

This was not the only way in which status affected careers. Before the 1960s most professions were hostile (or at best indifferent) to graduate entry. A degree seemed to offer few directly relevant skills which, even as late as the 1950s, was one reason why about one-half of all graduates ended up as teachers. Like trade unions, professions worried that their control over training, and hence entry, would be diluted, should they permit some aspects of it to be undertaken beforehand – at university. Since that era, graduate-only entry has become a sought-after status symbol of a would-be profession, marking for it a clear gap between its members and those non-graduates employed to assist them in conducting their work. Ever since the 19th century a long line of occupations has sought to acquire that status, including more recently nurses, and with some sections of the police force now wanting to follow suit. However, not only may graduate entry not generate higher earnings for a profession, it can fail to raise job status significantly, if at all. This was a mistake made, for instance, by British pharmacists in the 1950s and 1960s. They had "assumed that status, respect and prosperity would automatically follow from increased educational achievement, by making the profession degree entry only" (Anderson, 2001, p. 23). It made little difference to them. In this instance women were especially affected. They now constitute about 60 per cent of British pharmacists – a higher proportion than are lawyers, doctors or dentists – but their advance in educational qualifications and employment has not been matched fully by greater rewards of various kinds.

Educational credentials had been one, minor, aspect of Britain's earlier status hierarchy, but their reputation survived and was greatly enhanced intact, as that hierarchy was transforming. Thus, admission to what became known as "uni" – previously all post-secondary educational institutions had usually been referred to as "college" – remained a source of pride. Indeed, it was now more likely to be regarded as somehow superior compared with other ways of making a career. Furthermore, the enhanced social status of degrees facilitated the universities' transformation from being a tiny element in the education system to being, arguably, its main engine by the late 20th century. The construction of a positional economy of education, which is the subject of the next chapter, would have at its core the drive to obtain at least an undergraduate degree. Although only a minority of the population would still have a real opportunity to obtain one, the British education system would become structured around forms of testing that were geared towards entering "uni". Maximizing the chances of being admitted there would be affected not just by an adolescent's natural ability but also, indirectly, by money. Consequently, the major change in the role of Britain's status hierarchy would not lead to a more egalitarian framework of opportunities.

Education, money and class

Until the 1950s and 1960s, schooling was simply a waiting room for many middle- and upper-class children; it was where they became older so that a suitable job could then be found for them. While there, they had to acquire a certain minimum level of academic skills to be employable at all in non-manual work, but in many careers advanced skills were not needed. When necessary, these would be acquired later during employment. Many private schools to which these children were sent operated on small budgets, offered poor education and, often in the case of boarding schools, provided primitive living conditions for children.[8] Consequently, although private schooling could be afforded only by a minority of middle-class families, it was not that expensive. By the century's end, however, virtually all private schools secured their reputations through academic performance, and boarding facilities veered towards the lavish. Parents were now paying to have their children get the best possible educational credentials, to facilitate entry into the most prestigious universities. Grandparental financial contributions had become similarly important in facilitating this access route to the higher reaches of the job market (Chan and Boliver, 2013). From their launch pads, they would have the best chances of recruitment to lucrative and interesting jobs. The annual fees of the most renowned boarding schools now amounted to about one and a half times the net annual income of the average British family. Thus, despite a large growth in real family income during the second half of the 20th century, fewer than 7 per cent of children are attending fee-paying schools today. Indeed, especially after 1990, fee increases pushed them beyond the means of some occupations where private education had been common, with medical doctors being prominent among those who were losing out. Moving to the catchment area of the best state schools, or extra-school private tuition, increasingly became a much-used alternative for those whose finances precluded private schooling.

A variety of social changes had altered how class operated in Britain. Long-term transformation in the economy and the labour market produced massive occupational restructuring. White collar workers were no longer a minority surrounded by a large manual working-class majority. Even by the 1930s new skills and new technologies were beginning to extend the middle class well beyond its early-century heartland.[9] It became a far larger class by 2000 – constituting a clear majority of the population – and more diverse than it had been. Correspondingly, the working class shrank – absolutely as well as relatively. Many traditional skills became redundant in a de-industrializing economy. In addition, various sources of employment for the semi-skilled and unskilled – stevedores, navvies, railway porters and the rest – declined or disappeared. Yet the less skilled sectors of the labour market have never faced terminal decline, and some of them, including social care, continue to grow rapidly. Speculation, which began originally in the 1950s and which continues apace now, that most manual tasks would have been taken over by robots within decades might be countered by an alternative view of the future: a new age of domestic service. For example, data from the US Bureau of Labour Statistics a few years ago showed that the two fastest growing occupations in America were "personal care aide" and "health care aides", trends evident in nearly all advanced economies (Michaels, 2013).

This persistence of less skilled jobs is of major significance because it exposes a major flaw in much popular understanding of social mobility in Britain. The downsizing of that sector of the labour market was not a process that could last forever, with every worker eventually becoming highly skilled. Yet, by the end of the 20th century a false belief was infusing public policy that, if the work skills of all adolescents were raised, the demand for those skills would rise correspondingly. Economic growth would follow. Pursuing what was taken to be the model of California's Silicon Valley, it formed the basis for massive university expansion. Unfortunately, while that demand did rise, its growth was much lower than that of the graduate population. This had major implications for any strategies designed to create upward social mobility. Increasing the numbers with advanced educational credentials would not eventually make everyone high earners, or even securely middle class, because overall demand for highly skilled labour simply could not keep up with the growth in the number of graduates.

Linked to this was just how relatively important money had now become in sustaining patterns of inequality over time. It was the gatekeeper to initial opportunities in the labour market in a way that it had not been decades earlier. Money could supplement a child's ability and hard work in various ways that helped them obtain better credentials than their rivals. Although not all working-class families were effectively excluded from this educational market, most were. For those born into the working class, the educational system had been transformed into an obstacle to their social mobility. Major educational reorganizations, such as the widespread switch to comprehensive schools in the 1960s and 1970s, did virtually nothing to increase social mobility. Nor did the expansion of higher education achieve that (Blanden and Machin, 2004). As, for example, a major study of Scotland demonstrated, the marked, long-term, upward social mobility there was the product of changes in labour markets and in social structures, and not educational policies (Iannelli, 2011). This conclusion is supported by other data more generally for Britain (Goldthorpe, 2016, pp. 101–106). Relative social mobility remained much as it had always been: it had not increased initially and then declined later (Goldthorpe, 2012). Outside the United States, Britain now has the lowest social mobility in the Western world (Major and Machin, 2018). British education today has an important new role: that of helping to preserve social stasis.

Obviously, having a lot more money than the poor continues to enable the affluent to buy particular kinds of medical care, permits them to invest in private pension schemes, allows them to live in a less polluted environment, and facilitates their buying their own homes. Yet, arguably the most important change in the role of money for them lies elsewhere. It is as a replacement for family connections in providing indirect access for their children to the upper sectors of the labour market, doing so mainly via educational credentials. Across the political spectrum inequality of opportunity is criticized by politicians publicly. Unfortunately, most still hide behind the false assertion that the problem is caused primarily by institutional failure: underperforming state schools, universities that fall short in doing enough to diversify their intakes, and so on. Whatever their weaknesses, between them there is relatively little that these "whipping boys" could ever do to radically change the underlying situation. The problem lies in the dominant social incentives facing the more affluent: to obtain the "best" educational credentials possible for their children, and to deploy their resources in support of that. Institutional reforms, designed to improve educational performance, cannot alter the logic of the incentive facing those individuals and families and which underpin social stasis. That incentive is to keep ahead of others.

Notes

1 "Social engineering" is usually invoked against proposals intended to remove or reduce unwarranted or unfair advantage in some form of competition – such as in entry to an

elite university. Those proposals are no more "engineered" than are the social arrangements or procedures that gave rise to the advantages in the first place. Yet somehow the latter are assumed be "natural", perhaps being the hand of God or the result of natural selection, and not the product originally of human action, choice, design or acquiescence.

2 As Runciman pointed out in his early 1960s study, a curate and a bookmaker were not social equals. (The curate would always be socially superior, although the bookmaker might well earn much more.)
3 Although the "respectable" were more likely to be skilled, the fit between these two dimensions within the working class was far from complete, of course. Being "respectable" related to personal habits and behaviour and also the family's "moral" values.
4 After five continuous years following graduation of not having a job for which a degree is required, their entry into that sector of the labour market becomes less likely. They are in a very different situation from those just taking a "gap year" on graduating.
5 In 1937, 27.6 per cent of all pupils left between the ages of 14 and 16, with "the number of these paying fees being 4.8 per cent greater than the number paying no fees". The former pupils were mainly middle class and the latter working class.
6 Servants were supposed to take their behavioural cues from their employers. Even as late as 1960 the prosecuting barrister in the "Lady Chatterley's Lover" trial could address the jury with a question that became notorious – whether Lawrence's novel was something "that you would wish your wife or servants to read?".
7 For example, late 20th century jokes about so-called "chavs" and "Essex girls" point to some continuing strength for notions of class-based social superiority and inferiority and of differences of taste – in clothing, speech and many other ways.
8 These sorts of schools were often depicted in English novels, as with Evelyn Waugh's Llanabba School in *Decline and Fall*. However, the anti-intellectualism of such institutions was not evident in all private schools and their diversity should not be underestimated, as is discussed, for example, in Reed (1964).
9 Technological developments also created new industries – such as car manufacturing – in which better paid manual jobs were evident during the middle decades of the century. By the 1960s these workers were the subject of a major sociological study; see Goldthorpe, Lockwood, Bechhofer, and Platt (1968).

References

Anderson, Stuart (2001). "The Historical Context of Pharmacy", in Taylor, Kevin and Harding, Geoffrey (eds.), *Pharmacy Practice*. London: Taylor and Francis.

Blanden, Jo and Machin, Stephen (2004). "Educational Inequality and the Expansion of UK Higher Education", *Scottish Journal of Higher Education*, 51(2), pp. 230–249.

Chan, Tak Wing and Boliver, Vikki (2013). "The Grandparents Effect in Social Mobility: Evidence from British Birth Cohort Studies", *American Sociological Review*, 78(4), pp. 662–678.

Devine, Fiona (2004). *Class Practices: How Parents Help their Children Get Good Jobs*. Cambridge: Cambridge University Press.

Goldthorpe, John H., Lockwood, David, Bechhofer, Frank, and Platt, Jennifer (1968). *The Affluent Worker: Industrial Attitudes and Behaviour*. Cambridge: Cambridge University Press.

Goldthorpe, John H. (2012). *Understanding – and Misunderstanding – Social Mobility in Britain: The Entry of the Economists, the Confusion of the Politicians, and the Limits of Educational Policy*. Oxford: Barnett House Social Research Papers.

Goldthorpe, John H. (2016). "Social Mobility in Modern Britain: Changing Structure, Constant Process", *Journal of the British Academy*, 4, pp. 89–111.

Iannelli, Cristina (2011). "Educational Expansion and Social Mobility: The Scottish Case", *Social Policy and Society*, 10(2), pp. 251–264.

Major, Lee Elliot and Machin, Stephen (2018). *Social Mobility and Its Enemies*. London: Pelican Books.

McKibbin, Ross (1998). *Classes and Cultures: England 1918–1951*. Oxford: Oxford University Press.

Michaels, Walter Benn (2013). "Believing in Unicorns", *London Review of Books*, 7 February.

Norman, Paul, Gregory, Ian, Dorling, Danny, and Baker, Allan (2008). "Geographical Trends in Infant Mortality in England and Wales, 1970–2006", *Health Statistics Quarterly*, 40, pp. 18–29.

Nozick, Robert (1974). *Anarchy, State and Utopia*. New York, NY: Basic Books.

Office of National Statistics (2013). *Full Report – Graduates in the UK Labour Market*. Office of National Statistics.

Reed, John R. (1964). *Old School Ties: The Public Schools in British Literature*. Syracuse, NY: Syracuse University Press.

Runciman, W. G. (1966). *Relative Deprivation and Social Justice: A Study of Social Attitudes to Social Inequality in Twentieth-Century Britain*. London: Routledge and Kegan Paul.

Sandel, Michael (2012). *What Money Can't Buy: The Moral Limits of Markets*. London: Allen Lane.

Spens Report (1938). *Report of the Consultative Committee on Secondary Education with Special Reference to Grammar Schools and Technical Schools*. London: HMSO.

3

POSITIONAL COMPETITION

The key feature of the competition for educational credentials today is that it is *positional* competition – a form of competition that necessarily creates inequality. This feature is uncontroversial when participation is voluntary, imposing no costs on those who choose not to, and when all participants have comparable access to the resources that facilitate success. Neither condition is present in the competition for educational credentials in Britain, where obtaining the best credentials available is often a requirement for recruitment to the most desirable occupations. These are the jobs that are either intrinsically interesting or well remunerated, or both. Unfairness in access to the upper reaches of the labour market is not the only criticism made of this pursuit of credentials. For example, advocates of so-called "liberal education" – that education should concentrate on developing various aspects of a person's intellectual skills so that they can better enjoy a satisfying life – are strongly opposed to credentialism. However, the focus of this book is on inequality, and these other limitations are not discussed here.

The idea of positional competition

Traders in a large street market engage in competition with one another, as do clubs in football's Premier League. However, are their interactions identical? Or is the same term, "competition", concealing a fundamental difference? In both cases the presence of others – traders in one case, clubs in the other – constrains them. When selling the same product, traders cannot stray too far from one another in the prices they charge customers; when doing so, they would either make few sales or earn less than they could. If all charge the market price, all can acquire enough money to cover their various costs, including that of their own labour. One trader making a normal profit does not prevent others doing the same; this is the basic theory. Competition in a football league, or in, say, a squash ladder, is radically different.

The entire purpose of these activities is to win – to do better than the others, so that you rank higher than them in that league (or ladder). One team can improve its league position only if at least one other does worse. Competition is for position, and it is therefore necessarily zero-sum; the sum of all improvements in position equals the sum of losses made by others. Thus, positional competition intentionally creates unequal outcomes, a succinct definition of it being that it is competition for relative position within a hierarchy. Discussion of this separate notion of competition began in the late 1970s, but initial interest in it then diminished when it became clear that, as originally conceived, many of its supposed exemplars were instances of other aspects of competition (Hirsch, 1977; Ellis and Kumar, 1983).

Most positionally competitive hierarchies are voluntary. People usually participate in amateur sport because they enjoy the stimulus of trying to win. Businesses start professional leagues, paying players to participate, to generate income from the spectacle of individuals (or teams) going head to head in the pursuit of victory. When participation is voluntary, the inequalities that this positional competition generates are not unjust nor otherwise morally objectionable. The kinds of case that moral philosophers, such as Scanlon (2018), have mounted against inequality are simply irrelevant here. By contrast other hierarchies differ in that participation in them is either involuntary or imposes substantial costs on non-participants. They are open to various criticisms, not least because the outcomes they produce can be socially unjust. Social class in 20th century Britain was an example of this. It was a society where status was central to the class system, a key characteristic of status being that:

> "When everybody is somebody, then nobody is anybody". There is no limit to the growth of affluence, but social ranking is capped: room at the top is scarce, whatever the level of affluence.
>
> *(Offer, 2007, p. 233).*

This British system encompassed everyone, dominating social relations and politics. A much-cited observation, that "Class is the basis of British party politics; all else is embellishment and detail", was one way of stating succinctly what was obvious to all (Pulzer, 1967, p. 98). Unquestionably social status in Britain had the main features of positional competition, although how someone could try to improve their position was usually not obvious.

A central feature of more overt systems of positional competition is that, *ceteris paribus*, to restore your formerly high position when it has been taken by a competitor, you must do more than you did previously and also more than they did then. That "more" might be being fitter or more strategic or acquiring more information than them or spending more – depending on the context. There is a spiral to this form of competition, which, unless checked by either natural or artificial factors, is continuous. There might be side benefits to the spiral which offset the greater total expenditures (of various kinds) made by everyone, but, when there are not, it is a form of social waste. In some situations, all might have spent more to improve their own positions but end up exactly where they were previously. Of course, whether ultimately the pursuit of the inequality inherent in positional competition is nonetheless socially beneficial, or otherwise, is irrelevant to the decisions being made by the competitors.

Status hierarchies within a society are usually not someone's invention, but the side effect of a process or an unforeseen development. Once in place, and in producing winners as well as losers, the winners have every incentive to do what they can to preserve their advantage. This is true of competition for educational credentials in Britain. Today people compete to obtain higher-level qualifications than others, or higher-quality ones than theirs, and, more recently, to obtain them from institutions with higher status or reputations. They do so because, in general, the better jobs are usually obtained by those with formal qualifications that are *in some respect* "superior". Nevertheless, if you do not have the various resources to do well against others in this competition, you have little incentive to compete seriously at all. At the very least, a large minority of British adolescents are in that situation, and there are few alternative routes for them to the higher reaches of the British labour market. Even for those who do compete, the playing field is far from level.

It was not always like this, because Britain's social hierarchy was preserved earlier by other means. The competitive pursuit of credentials emerged during the second half of the past century, and, in stages, British education became increasingly subject to positional competition, first between individuals, and later also between educational institutions. While other countries have experienced similar developments, the British practice of competition for credentials is an extreme version of the phenomenon. Just as the older class system in Britain was often regarded as extraordinarily well defined, so too is its modern variant.

Over a period of decades several factors were crucial in its development and in its later modification. Systems of comparable educational credentials had to be established, so that relatively objective criteria about candidates for jobs were available to employers or to institutions offering still higher educational qualifications. At first, these systems were designed to identify those who were proficient in academic skills. They then became transformed into a means of, in effect, crudely rank ordering those who were proficient at a given level. This arose because employers now faced incentives to try to recruit the supposedly best qualified applicants, rather than the merely proficient. In Britain, positional competition would take the extreme form that it did because, unlike other countries, major alternative paths to these valued credentials had not emerged previously. In its final manifestation, competition was partly transformed away from one in which individuals simply worked towards the best higher educational credentials that they could possibly obtain. Instead, they were now competing to obtain, first, outstanding credentials from the most prestigious institutions but then also to acquire yet more credentials. The former objective emerged not because a new era of social snobbery had re-entered the British class system, but because the credibility of a formerly nationwide credentials' system had become subject to serious erosion in the late 20th century. In their pursuit of the "best", employers then had to supplement the information yielded by credentials themselves. This too would work to the advantage of those already well placed to secure entry into the higher levels of the labour market, making it still more difficult for their rivals.

Credentials that facilitate ranking

Competition in the hiring process could emerge fully only when evaluating levels of skills attained in education or training moved away from assessing overall proficiency *per se* to credentials identifying different levels of competence. At the beginning of the 20th century there had been no provision whatsoever in the education system for testing even proficiency, and no general credentials that adolescents could present to employers as proof of their current skills. For boys leaving school early to enter apprenticeships in industry, firms had often relied on age at departing school as an indicator of their possessing sufficient competence in academic skills. Engineering companies did this, for instance (Thelen, 2004, p. 122). For older adolescent boys, entry into both apprenticeships demanding advanced skills and universities depended on passing a special examination set by the organizations themselves. Before 1918, and for both that small minority leaving school at 18 and those leaving at 16, there was no British counterpart to American high school graduation. This changed, albeit slowly, with the introduction of the Higher School Certificate (HSC) and School Certificate (SC) in 1918. While both qualifications were always open to girls, even fewer girls than boys had an incentive to obtain them because of formal and informal restrictions on their access to the most skilled labour markets.

One advantage SC and HSC had over the American model was that testing and evaluation were undertaken by agencies attached to universities, and not by the individual schools themselves. Although not a nationally controlled system, standards varied little between these different examination boards. None had a direct incentive to lower their own standards and a powerful one to maintain their professional reputations. Comparability between students at different schools, and between those examined by different boards, became established. From its inception, the SC was essentially a test of the overall academic competence of a 16-year-old grammar school pupil, and that information was important for the upper echelons of the labour market.

Although it contained features permitting crude means of comparing some of those who obtained the qualification, the main principle of the SC was binary: a pupil either passed (and obtained the certificate) or failed (and did not).[1] Different subjects were examined separately, but only a single all-embracing mark was calculated when determining whether a pupil had passed. It was obtaining the certificate that really mattered. After 1951 this began to change slowly with the introduction of the General Certificate of Education (GCE) Ordinary (O) and Advanced (A) levels, the SC and HSC's successors.

Initially the proposal had been to have both O and A levels awarded only on a pass/fail basis, but that plan was not adopted (Petch, 1953, p. 168). Instead, and in several stages, the SC's essentially "proficiency" principle was replaced by a form of ranking. By the end of the century, with the O level itself having been replaced by the General Certificate of Education (GCSE), comparing relative individual performances would be one of the principal elements of British secondary education. Especially with the increased importance of A levels as academic credentials, how many passes a child obtained at both O and A levels, and at what grades, became a major determinant of their possible future.

In some respects, the charge towards credentialism was led by A levels and the universities. Students passed (or failed) individual subjects at A level, with different levels of performance (grades) being awarded officially. During the 1950s increased demand for the few places available in universities meant that relative performance at A level had to be used as one factor in deciding who would be admitted.

With O levels the change happened more gradually. Like A levels, students passed (or failed) in individual subjects, rather than a single pass awarded on overall performance. For several years this had the public appearance of being akin to the old SC in being essentially a pass/fail system, testing individual proficiency and not relative performance. Although different grades of pass and fail were awarded (initially percentages were used), until the 1960s they were not stated on the candidate's formal document, the certificate. Only the candidates themselves and their schools received that information and, thus, it was unavailable to employers directly. However, that they were graded from the beginning would open the way later to informal ranking. By the 1960s, how good a pass had been achieved in each subject was starting to matter much more. The merger from 1988 of O levels with the separate and, more recent, Certificate of Secondary Education (CSE) examinations merely confirmed that competence had been abandoned for a system which facilitated a rough form of rank ordering. The grading system has been changed on several occasions since then, currently having ten grades, of which only one is regarded as an outright failure. It is geared towards admission to further study, with the lower grades providing little relevant information with which to discriminate between applicants for relatively unskilled jobs.

A parallel switch, from signifying competence to ranking, occurred in higher education. Until the 1960s obtaining a Pass, or Ordinary, degree identified a graduate's proficiency, and was not an indicator of having performed less well than someone receiving an Honours degree. It signalled merely that its holder had for some reason, usually the cost of an additional year at university, decided not to engage in further study for Honours. The earlier, long-established, division of an Honours degree into separate classes had been designed for a specific purpose. This was to distinguish between different levels of originality demonstrated by examinees, rather than, for example, being an evaluation of how much each knew. To all but a few employers of graduates, of course, originality was of little interest, so that the Honours degree had mattered primarily within the university community itself, and often not even there.[2] As late as 1950 in Scotland – where the Ordinary degree was the equivalent of an English Pass degree – the proportion of students taking that degree was still 69 per cent of the total (Paterson, 2003, p. 162). Nevertheless, because Honours degrees had always been classified, they provided the foundation for a switch to a kind of ranking system in which undergraduate performance could be graded, from outstanding to minimally competent.

For employers, the information yielded by the Honours classification system was always somewhat limited, just as O and A level grades were. Necessarily some similarly talented students would fall just one side of the class boundary and some the other. Because there were so few differences in ability between individuals clustered in each sector of the achievement spectrum, a student with a low 2.1 might have been just as able as someone with a relatively high 2.2. Furthermore, many employers would be looking for attributes other than analytic skills when hiring, so academic ranking could be given less weight in the search for the "best". Yet, for all these limitations, it was a system that would facilitate crude attempts to rank individuals. Initially, though, the pressures to compete still more intensely in the positional economy of education were limited. A second development altered this.

The incentive to identify "the best"

From the mid-20th century there was a transformation in the scale of many British businesses and in the resulting incentives that now faced individual employers and employees. Previously the British economy was institutionally "bottom heavy", in the sense that it included proportionately more locally based firms and relatively few truly international ones. Indeed, one important interpretation of the development of British capitalism was its failure to innovate with corporate forms early and, instead, to persist with "personal capitalism", a mode based on family firms (Chandler, 1990). Smaller firms had fewer resources to try to find the "best" employees, and for them it was rational to satisfice when recruiting. Since many competitors were in a similar situation there was no pressure to abandon long-established hiring practices. Thus, in the years 1918–1950:

> The English labour market was still largely based upon many local economies – some of them very small ... These local economies were in turn still dependent on networks of intimate social relationships which permitted people to "speak for" each other and converted the networks themselves into informal labour exchanges.
>
> *(McKibbin, 1998, pp. 119–120 and p. 123).*

Subsequently local firms tended to give way to national ones, with some then being absorbed into international companies. This affected recruitment to both the most skilled positions and those in the middle range. A typical example of the long-term shift in scale was small firms of local solicitors which, through mergers from the 1970s onwards, became far larger and covered a greater territory in their business than their constituent firms had. Increased size contributed to a related development: the expanded firms were more likely to attempt to maximize profit margins. This helped to create a new consensus that it was no longer acceptable to appoint the merely proficient applicant. Only those who might keep the firm as competitive as possible ("the best") should now be selected.[3]

Absence of segmentation in education

In Britain individual students, and later educational institutions, became entwined in competitions for position. However, competition against everyone else occurs only when it is a single set of credentials that is valued, or where one set of credentials is widely valued far more highly than others. The British case is an outlier in this regard. In Britain's main competitors more "segmented" systems of credentials had developed from the beginning of the 20th century. Although they were very different from one another, in both Germany and the United States "segmented" forms of education and training emerged, restricting the effects of positional competition.

The basis for German segmentation was an early division between technical schools and traditional academic schools. The system was frequently credited with enhancing long-term German success in the development of its engineering-related industries – at least until the last decades of the 20th century. The German model was much admired by Lloyd George, who after the First World War, claimed that "The most formidable institution we had to fight in Germany was not the arsenals of Krupp … but the schools of Germany" (Jones, 1982, pp. 42–43). Although there had been some junior technical schools in England earlier in the century, Britain never really developed that model; even by 1937 there were few such schools. Arguably, before the Second World War this form of functional segmentation was unfeasible for Britain, and by that time the die was largely cast (Banks, 1955, p. 113fn.). The "number of first-class technical schools built between 1902 and 1918 [could] almost be counted on the fingers of … two hands". Most of "the organized science schools [re-emerged] … as institutions almost indistinguishable from … grammar schools" (Lowndes, 1937, pp. 192–193).

The British emphasis on academic study, especially by humanities' teachers, and the widespread assumption that this should be protected at all costs, would persist even when it became still more evident that introducing other educational "segments" might have advantages.[4] Academic study enjoyed unrivalled high status, both within the working class and at the apex of British society. For the former, education was the early 20th century route out of the working class, while the British political elite and its university leaders were closely linked. Although reduced in intensity, the bias towards the humanities persisted as a widely held social ideal for much of the century, and the traditional British model of how to organize post-secondary school education and training would survive.

The Labour movement too played an important role in limiting the introduction of a "technical segment". Until the Norwood Report of 1943 proposed technical schools as the third branch of a tripartite secondary education system, the idea of linking post-elementary education to preparing pupils for entry into various trades or professions was ignored by the Labour movement. It had little interest in that kind of scheme, partly from a belief that control of training for entrants into a trade was vital to the long-term survival of union membership and wage levels. While few imagined that schools would take over key stages of training traditionally undertaken on the shop floor, fear that some relevant skills might become part of a technical education in schools was regarded as a potential threat to the autonomy of any craft. Although tripartism would fail throughout the country, largely because of lack of resources, it was notably absent in areas of trade union strength, including in Wales, "where separate technical provision was virtually non-existent in its school systems" (Jones, 2002, p. 353).

Of course, segmentation in an educational and training system need not be functional in form. In the United States, its basis was geographical, involving different territories rather than different types of education. By contrast, in Britain positional competition in education could become so intense partly because there was just a single, national, ladder of competition. With the exceptions of Scotland (and Northern Ireland), at least initially, there were no truly separate ladders based on specific regions, territories or provinces. While there is also a national ladder of academic status in the United States, embracing universities such as Harvard, Yale and Stanford at its apex, it is not the only one. Especially within states far removed from areas in which the national elite institutions are located, there are local universities that can provide similar or even more secure entry into local and regional employment markets. Thus, credentials from Texas Tech have much greater esteem in Texas than would qualifications from universities of similar national prestige have in any region of Britain. Federalism plays a role in this, but it is not the only factor mitigating some of the effects of national positional competition. In addition, the American form of segmentation has been reinforced by educational structures that provide for greater accessibility to higher education. A more diverse set of arrangements made this possible. They included both two-year programmes in junior colleges, and also the transferability of course credits from one institution to another. This kind of flexibility partly limited the competitive intensity of a kind found in Britain. It was easier for students in the United States to enter, exit and re-enter educational programmes.

The net result was that, in the absence of either functional or territorial segmentation, the way was wide open for a more thoroughgoing positional economy in Britain's educational system during the late 20th century than in either Germany or America. However, at that point, the relationship between credentials and employment opportunities in Britain altered yet again.

The debasement of the credentials' "currency"

During the 1990s a major change began in the system of British academic credentials, a change that might be described as either inflationary or a debasement of the credentials' "currency". Far more high grades were being awarded at A levels, as were the higher classes of degrees at universities. Both affected how access to the labour market operated. Because of the former, universities now had even less evidence with which to distinguish reliably between those applying for places on courses. Moreover, university expansion was largely incompatible with their supplementing the evidence yielded by credentials with labour-intensive methods, including interviewing (a practice common in the 1960s). As for graduates in the job market, those with good degrees now had a much-expanded set of competitors with similar qualifications.

Consequently, in both the top and the bottom ranges of academic achievement, it had become even more difficult to distinguish between individuals. Originally, the distribution of the four classes of Honours degree (First, 2.1, 2.2 and Third) was "normal"; that is, it typically resembled the distribution along a bell-shaped curve, although quotas for each class were not used.[5] About half of all degrees were in the 2.2 class, with few Firsts, only about 20 per cent of the total being 2.1's and the rest Thirds. This is what would be expected when the performance of large numbers of students was being evaluated, with infrequent outstanding performances being distinguished from the ordinary and the latter from the weak. As early as the mid-1990s this "gold standard" in the awarding of degrees was being undermined, with degree classification increasingly becoming a debased currency. It was not until the second decade of the 21st century, though, that criticism of the inflation became intense. Even then critics tended to compare the situation not with the 1990s, but merely with 6 or 7 years earlier – a period when it was already well advanced.

No longer a bell-shaped curve, the distribution of degrees was inflated at the top end of the range, with the 2.1 degree replacing the 2.2 as the degree awarded to the typical student. So common during this century, it could no longer serve as a marker of special merit in the job market. The "currency debasement" continues apace. By 2017 three-quarters of all graduates received either First class or 2.1 degrees, with ten universities now awarding Firsts to between 30 and 42 per cent of all their graduates. Nor were the leaders in this movement those universities with the highest international reputations, universities that might be expected to attract outstanding students. Of those ten universities, only five were members of the 20-strong Russell Group, the organization of elite, research-oriented, universities (HESA, 2018).

Employers could now have less confidence that different universities were still using the same criteria in evaluating achievement. Partly because of the great increase in student numbers, the older arrangements whereby examiners from other universities enforced rigorously something akin to a national standard became far less effective. Now largely figureheads, with little incentive to insist on maintaining standards partly because they were paid so little, external examiners became marginalized. This enabled all universities to start relaxing their standards. To be competitive in recruiting students, especially from overseas, they had to follow a debasement policy because awarding too many poor degrees would limit their graduates' opportunities in labour markets. At first it was only academics, especially those who had been external examiners, who recognized this development, but more recently it became publicized persistently in the popular press. A race to the top for individual universities was, as the *Daily Telegraph* put it in June 2018, really a "race to the bottom" for the entire sector. This decline in comparable standards between universities would generate adverse outcomes for some students.

For employers, one of the main consequences was that it became far more difficult for them to differentiate between candidates' formal credentials – their degree class. The task of reducing a vast number of applications to a manageable shortlist for a job was made increasingly complex, because too few potential appointees could be filtered out early. Other criteria were needed, even before the "non-intellectual" skills that someone might bring to a job were considered. For graduates, therefore, to make it onto a shortlist required that they differentiate themselves from fellow competitors. One solution was for students to attend the most prestigious university available to them, rather than necessarily the one most suitable for their specific academic interests. The more prestigious their university, the more "doors" the graduate could prise open in the labour market. Employers would perceive graduates of highly ranked universities as not merely possessing the skills required for entry there in the first place, but having had to perform better than most of their peers to have gained it.

From the mid-1980s both employers and students were aided in identifying a rank ordering of prestige among universities, first by various surveys and, later, by formal assessment exercises. Education and research were put on a path to becoming markets, with universities competing to attract both students and research grants, as well as in the pursuit of research excellence. Yet, as markets in education, they lacked two key features for prospective students. There was no price competition because, even when fees were introduced, these were capped. In addition, there was virtually no reliable information for the vast majority of applicants as to the likely financial value of the courses open to them. As consumers, they were in the position of buying the proverbial pig in a poke. However, at their disposal were increasing amounts of information about the reputations – for research and teaching – of each British university.

Information on the supposed relative performance of universities, in relation to research and teaching, helped to create a tighter status hierarchy among these institutions, one which had been far less pronounced earlier except for the primarily social status attached to Oxbridge. It gave applicants for university courses prompts which, while no substitute for data on the relative employability of graduates with credentials from one institution rather than another, might help them avoid pursuing the least valuable credentials. University choice became more about individuals attaching themselves to institutional status. For both prospective students and subsequent employers, institutional reputation now mattered. For the employer, the more highly ranked a university, the greater the likelihood that its "pool" of graduates would contain few of those whom the employer would regard as merely mediocre, or worse.

There are many ways, both direct and indirect, in which this *relative* institutional reputation can matter in the labour market. For example, at some minimum, leading employers will typically devote more resources to recruitment fairs, and other hiring activities, at universities with the highest reputations. They do this because the largest proportion of outstanding applicants will be graduates from those institutions, and this helps minimize the risk of their hiring those regarded as mediocre or duds, as well as eliminating unnecessary costs. Data clearly demonstrate that there is a strong correlation between graduating from a prestigious university and access to, and progression through, the labour market. There is not merely a difference between the Russell Group and other British universities but also a marked difference, too, within the former. The relative prestige of your university greatly affects your future prospects (Wakeling and Savage, 2015).

The most rigorous version of this employer strategy of institutional differentiation is to confine recruitment primarily to applicants who obtained their qualifications from institutions where even their lower ranked graduates can be expected to be exceptionally well qualified, by comparison with the typical potential applicant. For example, research in America provides clear evidence of how its elite employers systematically ensure that applicants graduating from universities which a firm does not regard as a "core" or a "targeted" institution are not treated as seriously as graduates from those that it does (Rivera, 2011, p. 76, and Rivera, 2015). This approach to hiring has been famously parodied in the popular television series *Suits* in which the Manhattan law firm will hire graduates only from Harvard's Law School.[6] Obviously, it is highly probable that there are even better candidates outside "core" institutions, but the impossibility of identifying them before the shortlisting stage means that attempting to do so would increase the risk that the "not-quite-so-good" might be shortlisted and even be appointed.

While effective, this highly selective approach to recruitment is more difficult to utilize in large firms, those immediately below the apex of the elite level, and those whose practices are subject to exceptional public scrutiny. For them especially, another way of filtering out some of the seemingly not-so-good is to give priority to those applicants who have more credentials. Consequently, there is now a much greater incentive to study for post-graduate degrees. Starting with those who had graduated from low-prestige universities, or who had poor First degrees, the imperative for becoming more competitive in the labour market via this route grew rapidly. As recently as the late 1970s relatively few graduates in Britain studied for a Master's degree or a PhD, but between 1996 and 2013 the proportion of working people in Britain with a post-graduate qualification rose from about 4 to 11 per cent of the total. Nevertheless, caution is essential when interpreting this growth. Some qualifications, including MBA programmes in Britain, partly involve outsourcing of elements of training processes that would have been undertaken informally by firms in-house in a previous era. In most cases, though, the additional knowledge and analytic skills developed in Master's programmes have added little, if anything, to the resources directly available to the subsequent employer. For the employer, however, giving some priority to those with post-graduate qualifications does reduce the proportion of weak graduates likely to be placed on long lists and then, later, on shortlists. It is another way of managing risk in recruitment. The assumption is that those who had been merely fortunate to obtain the kind of qualification they acquired at the undergraduate level might not be able to engage successfully with a second educational hurdle. Those who could might at the very least be demonstrating determination and a capacity for sustained work.

The single competitive ladder that the British education system had become, one now centred on credentials and institutional prestige, was extended by this growth in post-graduate education. It had major consequences for inequality in Britain, especially because it tended to undermine further the feasibility of equality of opportunity. Educational credentials were just another product in which money could be invested for future financial gain. Lower down the credentials ladder this was clearly evident. Considered together, expenditures on private education, additional tutoring, and moving home to districts with the best performing schools were being used more widely than earlier. They could help a child obtain the grades needed to enter the most prestigious universities.

In addition, whilst at university, students from more affluent families could take advantage of an increasingly common practice of companies offering unpaid internships during university vacations. Not only can an internship bolster a student's curriculum vitae, but in some cases it leads to full-time employment on graduation. Students from poorer families can less afford to forgo paid temporary employment during their vacations, and typically miss out on this. (For firms, internships have become a further filtering device in recruitment, given the paucity of *comparable* information about potential applicants.) For the affluent, money can then be available at a later stage for post-graduate courses. Studying for a graduate degree without sufficient funds would usually be impossible, an additional disadvantage to the student who has poor parents.

Consequently, today money drives the main mechanism for sustaining future social inequality, the education system, in much the way that accident of birth did a century ago. There is an obvious paradox here. For many decades during the 20th century, education was seen widely as a way in which some people would be able to overcome the disadvantages of being relatively poor. Since then the positional economy of education has enabled the education system to become the primary route over time for maintaining social advantage. Other factors then feed into this positional economy, providing further advantage for some and greater disadvantages for others. While financial resources shape inequality generally, through its impact on the education that a person can acquire, even with comparable educational qualifications, some social groups face additional barriers:

> While some groups do better than the white British majority, Pakistanis, Bangladeshis and black Africans suffer higher rates of unemployment, lower occupational status and lower earnings ... Such ethnic penalties remain even after controlling statistically for individual differences, for instance in respect of education.
>
> *(Brynin and Güveli, 2012, p. 574).*

It might be thought that this evidence indicates that contemporary employers are not really seeking the "best" when hiring. However, there is an alternative explanation, one that follows from the analysis of discrimination and income to be outlined in Chapter 4. Employers want the "best", but for several reasons there is nearly always insufficient information about individuals to identify that person. Frequently those recruiting have to use additional information, not directly about individuals themselves, to fulfil their remit. Among the consequences generated by this are "ethnic penalties". A fundamental information deficit means that the pursuit of the "best" tends both to fail in a large number of cases and to facilitate new forms of discrimination.

Notes

1 In the Joint Matriculation Board, for example, grades above the mere Pass level – called Good, Credit and Distinction – could be awarded in individual subjects and that information would appear on the certificate.
2 In 1931 my father received an Ordinary degree from Aberdeen University and a few weeks later a university scholarship to study for a PhD there.
3 The number of qualified solicitors doubled between 1983 and 2003, while at the same time the number of firms shrank. Even more important than this was change in the structure of firms, with the ratio of solicitors to non-fee-earning (support) staff altering, with proportionately far fewer of the latter being employed. The emphasis within firms was now much more directly on fee earning capacity, and inevitably this would affect how solicitors were recruited (Ackroyd and Muzio, 2007, pp. 731 and 733).
4 In 1959 the scientist and novelist C. P. Snow prompted a major public debate about Britain's bias towards the humanities following his Rede Lecture, "The Two Cultures". Although it coincided with new government policies enhancing science and technology teaching, the bias in British society identified by Snow was securely entrenched and, in part, persisted.
5 With a normal distribution there are more instances of the phenomenon at the centre than elsewhere, with the incidence falling away continuously towards the two extremes.
6 Except, in later series, the character portrayed by Meghan Markle.

References

Ackroyd, Stephen and Muzio, Daniel (2007). "The Reconstructed Professional Firm: Explaining Change in English Legal Practices", *Organization Studies*, 28(5), pp. 729–747.

Banks, Olive (1955). *Parity and Prestige in English Secondary Education*. London: Routledge and Kegan Paul.

Brynin, Malcolm and Güveli, Ayse (2012). "Understanding the Ethnic Pay Gap in Britain", *Work, Employment and Society*, 26(3), pp. 574–587.

Chandler, Alfred D. (1990). *Scale and Scope: The Dynamics of Industrial Capitalism*. Cambridge, MA: Belknap Press.

Ellis, Adrian and Kumar, Krishnan (eds.) (1983). *Dilemmas of Liberal Democracy: Studies in Fred Hirsch's Social Limits to Growth*. London and New York, NY: Tavistock.

HESA (2018). *Higher Education Student Statistics: UK, 2016/17 – Qualifications Achieved*. Department of Education, 11 January. Available at https://www.hesa.ac.uk/news/11-01-2018/sfr247-higher-education-student-statistics/qualifications

Hirsch, Fred (1977). *Social Limits to Growth*. London and Henley: Routledge and Kegan Paul.
Jones, Gareth Elwyn (1982). *Controls and Conflicts in Welsh Secondary Education, 1889–1944*. Cardiff: University of Wales Press.
Jones, Gareth Elwyn (2002). "Policy and Power: One Hundred Years of Local Education Authorities in Wales", *Oxford Review of Education*, 28(2–3), pp. 343–358.
Lowndes, G. A. N. (1937). *The Silent Social Revolution: An Account of the Expansion of Public Education in England and Wales, 1895–1935*. London: Oxford University Press, Humphrey Milford.
McKibbin, Ross (1998). *Classes and Cultures: England 1918–1951*. Oxford: Oxford University Press.
Offer, Avner (2007). *The Challenge of Affluence*: Oxford: Oxford University Press.
Paterson, Lindsay (2003). *Scottish Education in the Twentieth Century*. Edinburgh: Edinburgh University Press.
Petch, James A. (1953). *Fifty Year of Examining: The Joint Matriculation Board, 1903–1953*. London: George G. Harrap.
Pulzer, Peter G. J. (1967). *Political Representation and Elections: Parties and Voting in Great Britain*. New York, NY: Praeger.
Rivera, Lauren A. (2011). "Ivies, Extracurriculars, and Exclusion: Elite Employers' Use of Educational Credentials", *Research in Social Stratification and Mobility*, 29(1), pp. 71–90.
Rivera, Lauren A. (2015). *Pedigree: How Elite Students Get Elite Jobs*. Princeton, NJ: Princeton University Press.
Scanlon, T. M. (2018). *Why Does Inequality Matter?* Oxford: Oxford University Press.
Thelen, Kathleen (2004). *How Institutions Evolve: The Political Economy of Skills in Germany, Britain, the United States, and Japan*. Cambridge: Cambridge University Press.
Wakeling, Paul and Savage, Mike (2015). "Entry to Elite Positions and the Stratification of Higher Education in Britain", *The Sociological Review*, 63(2), pp. 290–320.

4

MERIT, MARKETS AND LUCK

In contemporary societies the main threads of explanation usually invoked in some form when explaining income inequality are merit, the logic of the market and luck. Typically, they are used in combination with one another in attempts at justifying these inequalities as well as when explaining them.

When citing merit as a justification for higher pay, it is often said to be appropriate for those who have more advanced skills than those possessing lesser ones or none at all. In the industrial era this was the main basis for pay differentials among skilled manual workers; how difficult it was to acquire or apply a specific skill, compared with other trades, was considered a factor when determining the "rate for the job". (Obviously, the skills in question are always ones relevant to the activities of that society, and not a mere capacity to do something that hardly anyone could ever use, need or value there.) Appointment by merit to jobs that require these skills involves, at the very least, appointing those who are demonstrably capable of doing the job competently – to the level required. A narrower version of what constitutes "merit" requires that those hired are not merely proficient, but that they are individuals who could perform the tasks better than anyone else available for employment. Moreover, depending on the task in question, "merit" not only may be identified with respect to technical abilities, but can include moral virtue or altruistic behaviour, for example. The major problem in utilizing merit in its narrow version is the reliability of possible evidence with which to compare those who have already demonstrated competence, as well as how reliable current evidence can be for future performance.

Most who defend income inequality as an inevitable consequence of how markets operate see distribution via this mechanism as being neutral. That is, markets are unbiased with respect to the outcomes for specific individuals, or to put it another way, there is an "absence of discrimination among customers or among suppliers" (O'Donnell, 1989, p. 39). Ultimately inequality in pay reflects the demand for and supply of specific kinds of labour, or at least it does so in the absence of state restrictions – including minimum wage laws and so on. That is the key idea. However, even in the absence of restrictive devices market neutrality does not mean that throughout all labour markets there is some kind of "balance" between demand and supply which sets *the* price for a particular kind of labour. Why?

The less skilled a job the more people there are who could do it. Although some will perform unskilled tasks better than others, differences in remuneration will arise only when the best performances add considerably greater value and when it is easy to identify those performances from others. Otherwise an overall market rate for that labour is established. Above this level the more skilled the job the greater become the variations in the value that employees can generate for their employer. When it is possible to identify different levels of performance, different levels of remuneration or a hierarchy of pay scales can be established. The size of the pay gap between individuals will depend on the demand for different levels of that skill and the number of potential suppliers at each level.

Yet when a very high level of skill is needed, and especially when a variety of these skills is required and performance of them has to be sustained over a long period, a major problem arises in the availability of information about different potential employees. This is the same problem as appointment on merit. How one candidate compares with another may matter to the employer, but establishing accurately the relative difference in their performances – and hence their value to a firm – becomes hard. While employers will want to pay more to attract the most skilled within this group, just how much more they should pay one candidate rather than another is unclear. (How much less should a team pay a goalkeeper thought to be the fifth or sixth best in the world than the one regarded as the best?) Uncertainty as to the size of the available labour supply at the precise level required makes it less likely that an overall market rate of pay will be established. Consequently variations in relative remuneration among the supposedly most skilled employees in the Britain, compared with those in lesser skilled jobs, are enormous because of this information deficit relating to supply.

Although frequently invoked in informal conversations, by those who believe that they are unlucky in their level of pay by comparison with others, luck rarely features in analyses of "who gets paid what, and why". Nevertheless, luck is not merely a basis of excuses for individual misfortune. It plays a substantive, though often overlooked, role in discussions of income distribution.

The main beneficiaries of good luck in the labour market often seek to deny its role, either by emphasizing that their rewards derive entirely from their meriting them or their being an inevitable consequence of market forces. Many of the highest paid believe their talent and long working hours warrant their level of remuneration (Toynbee and Walker, 2008). Thus, a frequent assertion is that their selection for a specific position follows directly from their being uniquely qualified to do it best. The employer is better off than it would be if someone else had been appointed, and their current high level of pay reflects that. On this reasoning, to recognize the elements of luck in being better off is seen as diminishing the strength of their claim to their level of remuneration. As will become evident shortly, in few cases could anyone ever provide direct evidence that they were indeed the better appointee, and more importantly, almost certainly many are not.

To understand this, it is useful to consider an especially illuminating example of a highly paid career in the United States for which there is a uniquely complete set of data. More than for virtually any other area of employment in the world, the relevant skill levels of those who might be appointed are known in great detail by all prospective employers, as is how long appointees then remain employed in the industry, and what happens to them subsequently. Furthermore, not only does each employer have a strong incentive to recruit the supposed "best", but the process of hiring them reveals publicly something akin to a rank ordering by experts of all possible employees – evidence lacking for other industries. It is possible to explore with great precision here the respective roles played by luck and merit in appointments to careers with large income inequality. This example is the recruitment of players to the National Football League (NFL) – by far the main employer of gridiron football players in the world. Unlike their coaches, most players are not white, and the sheer amount of information available to hirers about all possible recruits is one reason why discrimination on racial grounds can creep less into the hiring process overall than in most other forms of skilled employment.[1]

The data reveal that, even with more detailed information available than in most other recruitment processes, those selected to these highly skilled and high-paying positions were often not the "best" available. The fit between the rank ordering that the teams have when recruitment begins (as to who will be the "best" recruits) and the players' relative performance subsequently is much weaker than would be expected, given the level of information in the hands of employers. Inevitably, in other industries where much less is known by employers about potential recruits, this "fit" will be weaker still than it is with NFL footballers.

Luck, merit and the case of gridiron football

The amount of directly relevant comparative evidence on the quality of the work skills an individual could be expected to provide in the NFL is so large that any potential employee's skills can be compared in detail with all others. Their tasks as employees will be virtually identical to much of what all had done in the previous 8 years – at high school and then university.[2] During their university years, especially, much of their time will have been spent honing those skills, rather than in academic study. There are volumes of video, statistical and evaluative data available for each of them for at least their entire period as college footballers, and in many cases also for their performances at secondary school. Throughout their earlier "careers" those data are continuously analysed in detail by all NFL recruitment specialists.

The high financial stakes involved in employing any specific player provide a strong incentive for this.

The 32 employers (teams) in the NFL are each entitled to maintain a roster of 53 players, so that each season there are nearly 1700 of these jobs in the industry. The primary recruitment of newcomers is through an annual "draft" of seven rounds in which every team is entitled to choose, in order, during each round one player concluding their fourth year at university – with a total of 224 players being drafted annually.[3] In theory, therefore, during each successive round of drafting the best 22-year-olds still left in the draft will be selected. The outstanding players who then stay fit could have careers of 10 years and sometimes more, but the average career lasts only 6 years, so that the annual addition of seven players from the draft would be insufficient to fill a team's roster. One consequence of this is that, when needed, undrafted players also have to be hired each season. Barring injury, and given that there are more jobs available in the industry than there are draftees, it would be expected that most of the 224 drafted in any year – and most especially the first 32 – could be expected to have long careers.

This is a system that produces a hierarchy of perceived merit, based on a huge amount of evidence, and where the employee's own financial rewards relate directly to their own position in the hierarchy. Because players chosen in the draft are thought to be the best, all are offered lucrative contracts by the employer, with more being paid the higher the round in which a player is chosen. The very first player selected will typically have a contract worth nearly ten times more overall than those chosen from round 3 onwards ($28 million versus $2–3 million in 2016, for example)[4]. Consequently, it would be expected that, compared with players drafted in lower rounds, those selected in the highest rounds of each year's draft would have longer careers as established players in the NFL, and, indeed, overall they do. However, because the differences in relative ability are so small, a surprisingly large proportion of players selected each year do not develop long-term careers in the industry, and certainly not at its apex, the NFL. Most importantly for our purposes, this is true even of the first 32 draftees. With seven of the eight types of starting positions in a football team, the chances of a drafted player *not* becoming a regular starter on a team during their careers are high: for the top 32 this ranges from 30 to 42 per cent of the total (WesternChief, 2015). Thus, with each team having 22 starting positions, for a total of 704 overall, typically only about 21 of any given year's 32 first-round selections will become the occupants of those positions then or later.

The significance of this is obvious: even at the highly elite first-round stage, a large minority of teams could have done better by selecting someone else – *had they been able to know who that player was*. Given how much information employers have available for those selections, this is a relatively low level of success in recruitment and is evidence of a strong element of luck involved in drafting. Luck seems to be needed especially when choosing those playing in positions where the range of skills demanded is greater, and especially for the key position of quarterback. Indeed, significantly the one type of position, lineman, where there is a much higher probability that a first-round draftee will become a regular starter is arguably the one where the *range* of skills required is least.

Consequently, some players selected in lower rounds, or ones who had to become undrafted free agents, outlast many high draft picks in having an NFL career (Arthur and Binney, 2016). One result is that employing free agents is common, and has become more common, not just because of injuries to players but also because so many draftees do not fulfil earlier expectations of them. The role of luck for the individual player is clear here. Some were lucky to receive the initial high-value contracts that they did. Others, who were drafted in lower rounds or not drafted at all, but who would have long careers, were unlucky, in that at the start of their careers, they received less than their eventual worth compared with the "lucky" ones.

The relevance of luck here should not be misunderstood. Those early round draftees who failed to develop a career were indeed highly proficient gridiron footballers, but they turned out not to be as proficient in their job as some of their peers ranked lower by NFL teams. They were the beneficiaries of luck, because with any job estimating *relative* potential successfully is inherently inaccurate.

This point does not derive from any quirk in what some might think was an atypical industry. Rather, it exposes a crucial point for all skilled employment. Even with an exceptionally high level of relevant information, predicting who will be better than someone else in a particular job is extremely imprecise. Reduce the level of information below that available to the NFL employers, and the "fit" between potential and ultimate success among "competent" candidates will plummet. For any level of proficiency that is required, however high, it is much easier to identify the "proficient" than it is to rank order them. In addition, the more diverse the skills needed for a career, and the more open-ended they are, the less accurate will rank ordering prove. With NFL players, the skills needed for those playing in any given position can be clearly defined. With many other jobs, including senior executives in companies, the range is broader, with overall comparisons between candidates partly dependent on the weight accorded to each possible variable. Thus, assessing the likely value of a given candidate when recruiting a senior orthopaedic surgeon to a National Health Service Trust is typically easier than hiring its new chief executive.

The more important it is to try to determine who is better than whom – establishing a rank ordering via testing and evaluations – the greater the incidence of appointments that to some degree will prove "wrong". They are "wrong" in that a better appointment might have been made. Inevitably the result is a still greater role for luck, even than in the NFL, in determining who becomes the highest paid. Relative potential is always just potential, and it does not translate directly into relative future performance, irrespective of how rigorously the "baseline" of proficiency has been defined.

This is why so-called meritocratic selection is problematic even in the most limiting of cases. That is, in those instances when a vast amount is known about potential recruits, when employers believe that they need to know approximately how they rank against one another and when there is a strong incentive for them to select the best that they can. This point is scarcely surprising. With all skills, there are rarely any individuals – excluding the occasional Mozart and Wayne Gretzky – who display such exceptional ability, and an obvious capacity for learning and hard work, from an early age that they always rank far ahead of everyone else. (Historically, constraints on opportunities for girls were so great that those who displayed exceptional talent when older, such as Jane Austen, would have had few forums in which to reveal their ability previously.) Most who eventually turn out to perform a skill at a very high level have had at least some close competitors earlier who might have been the ones to become the best. As the economist Robert H. Frank (2016, p. 66) noted in an analysis of the role of luck in determining who becomes successful:

> … many extremely talented and hardworking people fail to achieve any significant material success. Many of them are simply less lucky than the winners.

Because testing and evaluations to create rank ordering are necessarily imprecise mechanisms, and often highly unreliable, luck inevitably plays a major role in determining who succeeds. Luck falls outside what could have been foreseen or could be controlled by the person concerned.[5]

When firms believe they must employ only the most skilful at some highly skilled activity, the remuneration of those hired to such posts is pushed upwards, even though many appointees will not later be considered among the best. For the employer, the "waste" involved in paying high wages for those who will then turn out this way could still be worthwhile, if enough of those chosen do prove successful. One way of effecting this is to payroll more young employees than currently needed and then to find ways of "testing" each of them over time. Some of the most well-financed football clubs, including Manchester City and Chelsea, do this by retaining on their books more players than they require; they then loan them to other major clubs where they acquire experience of regular first-team football. This is an unusual and very expensive way of limiting the risks with which an employer is faced when seeking to hire and then retain only the best. There are few other industries where the employer will not be disadvantaged by lending an employee to another firm, and where there is sufficient evidence on their performance with the latter so that a full evaluation about retaining them can be undertaken later.

Usually the advantage lies with employees, including "lucky" ones. The uniqueness of being identified (in many cases incorrectly) as being among the best on appointment increases the remuneration that all of them – those ultimately unsuccessful in the job for which they were selected as well as the successful – can command. Their bargaining position with respect to pay would be much weaker in a world of perfect information or one where relative performance mattered much less. The "lucky" in this respect might be considered modern exemplars of those "that have", of which it says in Matthew's Gospel: "to those that have shall be given".

The lower the level of proficiency required for a job the more employable people there are, so that rank ordering with any precision becomes increasingly difficult at such levels. That reduces the opportunity there for individuals to bargain with an employer. Consequently a level of pay is established, and prevails, at a market rate. What is usually called "rent-seeking behaviour" – that is, seeking excess remunerations as a condition for accepting a job offer – will nearly always be unsuccessful. Rent seeking can operate only when there is either a shortage of a particular skill or when there is an information deficit combined with a perceived incentive to appoint the supposed best. Most employees do not operate under these conditions.

Of course, employers could incur lower costs were they to establish a minimum required standard of proficiency for appointees, having set a suitably high bar for that, and then on their applications require all candidates to state the minimum level of overall remuneration they would accept if appointed. However, when employers believe both that they will lose out to competitors should they fail to employ the "best" and that they can identify the "best", this is not an option for them. Exaggerated faith by many of them in their ability to so identify is a major contributory factor to pay inflation at senior levels.

Especially in multi-skilled occupations, high earners are often not people who compare well with others, but those who cannot, with any accuracy, be compared directly with anyone. This is with respect to both their being the supposed "best" and their appropriate level of remuneration. A parallel with sports teams would be if the employer were having to recruit the "best", not from within just one sport, but from a wide range of sports. Similarly, because relatively poor performance in running an institution is difficult to evaluate in sufficient detail to satisfy an industrial tribunal, even the not terribly competent can secure satisfactory redundancy packages and lengthy tenure. The remuneration of high executives is usually a small proportion of total costs in many organizations, so that generous packages at their apex often pose few financial risks to them. A modern version of the 50-year-old Peter Principle, that people rise to the level of their own incompetence, might be that towards the apex of organizations employees rise to the level of their most generous possible redundancy package (Peter and Hull, 1969).

Some organizations, especially those where public or customer esteem matters as much as profit or sales, engage in behaviour that actually encourages rent seeking by appointees at the highest levels. In the higher education sector, for example, one cause of this is "the tendency of universities towards *isomorphism* (i.e. all seeking to be like each other) and *filiopietism* (i.e. all seeking to be like venerable institutions such as Harvard or Oxford" (Palfreyman and Temple, 2017, p. 124). This contributes to a belief that, to aspire to becoming a "venerable institution", its leadership has to be paid at least as much as those employed at venerable ones. It is not surprising, therefore, that neither of the two universities that prompted the greatest controversy over vice chancellor remunerations and severance payments in 2017 were among the 20 members of the elite Russell Group.

The internationalization of some labour markets has further raised the pressure to inflate pay in the most senior positions. This includes those recruiting from countries where beforehand a premium had been paid to individuals when trying to attract them to places that they might previously have dismissed as less desirable. Thus, while a lawyer or manager currently employed in, for example, China or the Gulf States might recognize that accepting a post in Britain would entail lower pay than their current job, their bargaining position could well be better than that of someone moving from within the United Kingdom. Their current high pay shapes how much below it a British employer would believe they could realistically offer without endangering acceptance of the job.

Nevertheless, it might be argued that the focus here on the relationship between *individual* merit and remunerations among the most highly skilled is only a secondary aspect of contemporary inequality. Irrespective of individual advantage and disadvantage in the labour market at that level, at least as important is the overall distribution of income in Britain. As we have seen, this distribution has become less equal in recent decades. Furthermore, it has been occurring in a country where, from the mid-1970s, the share of national income received by labour declined and that of capital rose correspondingly, so that during the first decade of this century it was at its lowest since the First World War (OECD, 2015, p. 15).

Obviously, major changes in public policy have made their contribution to altering the relative position of Britain's high and low earners. As noted in Chapter 1, for a decade after the late 1970s the highest earners generally increased greatly their remunerations in relation to those of the lower earners. One cause of this was the major change in tax rates introduced by the incoming Conservative government in 1979. In its first budget the highest rate of income tax was reduced from 83 to 60 per cent, and a further reduction to 40 per cent followed in 1988. (Britain was not alone in changing tax rates in this direction, that trend being evident in other OECD countries after the 1970s.) There has been no corresponding reversal of this development since then. Yet Thatcher's political initiative was only one factor though reshaping income distribution in Britain. There were also fundamental changes in how labour markets operated in this country and elsewhere. In this regard Britain in the 21st century is a very different place to what it was in the mid-20th century.

Structural change and labour markets

The gap between those who have high and those who have low net pay has increased, because of changes at both ends of the pay spectrum. At the low end, a crucial factor was the decline of trade unions in defending the interests of those employed in lower paid jobs. In turn, this was partly due to the transformation in the British economy after the 1960s. The relative decline of an industrial sector in which unions were long established, and its supplanting by a much-expanded service sector where they were not, reduced the scope and power of collective bargaining in the economy. As in the United States, a smaller proportion of the workforce is now unionized, and the core of the union movement in both countries is situated in the public sector.

At least in its initial stages, technological innovations can also weaken unionism, the rise of the so-called gig economy this century being a prime example of this. Apps on phones enable consumers and supposedly independent suppliers to be connected directly with each other – as with taxi and courier firms, which claim not to be the employers of those directly supplying those services. Their case is that they are the providers of a technology for those who supply and those using the service. This enables firms, like Uber, to avoid paying any benefits to their drivers, such as holiday pay, as a traditional taxi firm would, on the grounds that their drivers are self-employed. Obviously, the resulting increases in the low-earning, self-employed, sectors of the economy might not always be permanent. Legal action against the companies could partly reverse the initial downward pressure on earnings generated by technology-driven changes, but whether in the long run it would do so fully may be doubted.[6]

The decline in some industries of older, large, companies, and their replacement by new ones, has also had a major impact on union membership. The airline industry is one example. Former state airlines in Europe, such as British Airways, usually inherited a highly unionized workforce on privatization, and subsequent periodic conflicts with the unions did not eliminate them. However, the large growth in air travel during recent decades was not driven by these companies but by newer "no frills" firms, which minimized their costs partly by refusing recognition to unions. Eventually, the no-union policy of Ryanair would be breached, but not by action from its lower-paid employees. It was the much more highly remunerated pilots that did so. It is far from clear that less skilled workers in an industry would have the same leverage to force union recognition, thereby reducing pay differentials overall. Indeed, the pilots' case fits well with the British tradition of trade unionism. Historically, the British experience was characterized by early growth of unions based on specific skills, and for whom controlling the conditions under which those members worked was central (Thelen, 2004, p. 100). Unlike Germany, where unionization was founded on entire industries and not skills, less skilled workers in Britain became unionized only later.

This was not the only development in labour market structure contributing to the widening earnings' gaps. The demise of Britain's localized economies, discussed in Chapter 3, increased the importance of maximizing earnings' capacity within commercial organizations. In turn, it necessitated greater incentives than earlier to those seen as contributing most to the objective. A similar trend was evident in organizations that previously were little concerned with income generation, but which now had to raise substantial sums through quasi-commercial activities. British universities were one example of this. Earlier the pay of senior academics was constrained. Although professors' salaries were not on a fixed scale, as were those of more junior academics, there was a minimum which all had to be paid and an average for professorial pay to which each university had to conform. Consequently, no single university could have many highly paid professors, and this restricted pay inequality at the higher levels, just as national pay scales did so among junior academics. Today, constraints on high pay result solely from those of a university's total budget, and among academics overall there is greater income inequality at the higher levels than there used to be.

A further consequence of the demise of localized economies has been to provide conditions in which "winner-take-all" markets can thrive. Citing tax advice as an instance of such markets, Frank (2016, p. 10) argues that technological innovation enables the most skilled practitioners today to pull further ahead of their rivals than they could have done in the past. They can more easily dominate an industry, generating higher revenues, at the expense of rivals. This is akin to positional competition, where relative position matters. Here it is "dominating" others that is the prime goal for a firm. It can afford to pay more than others to recruit the seemingly "best" employees when expanding their business later, and thereby can preserve their dominant position.[7] The greater ability of some firms to dominate others affects remuneration at an industry's apex. The former are not paying some notional going rate for key employees, but, instead, pay whatever it takes to make sure that the supposed "best" people work for them and for no one else. (A similar strategy for domination has been evident in football, where the salaries and transfer fees paid by those in a financially dominant position – such as Barcelona, Real Madrid and Manchester City – have escalated in recent years.)

Nevertheless, this is not always a one-way process. In an industry where a firm had become so far ahead of potential challengers, its current power in recruiting the specialist labour required could enable it to start reducing its pay levels. The monopsony it has in that labour market could be used to increase its profits at the expense of employees. Whether it does so will depend partly on how much it believes it would be vulnerable to some further technological innovations from challengers who had themselves recruited sufficiently skilled employees at the now lower wage rates. In turn, the likelihood that subsequent innovation will draw on skills very similar to those of its current workforce, or alternatively on significantly different ones, becomes relevant in decisions about levels of pay.

If all these developments enable us to account for increasing inequality in income distribution, however, there is still an important element missing in the explanation. How are we to account for some social groups, especially women and racial minorities, often doing less well than white men, especially in some sectors of the labour market?

Discrimination and income inequality

With higher educational levels now, particularly for more skilled jobs, it would be expected that those engaged in recruitment would be less prone than their predecessors to discriminate against applicants on grounds that include, among others, sex, race, religion and obesity. There is clear evidence of a generational shift in Britain away from racial prejudice, and the highly educated are among those groups where this has been most rapid (Ford, 2008, p. 636). Yet, especially with respect to ethnic and racial minorities, studies of recruitment and promotion in labour markets continue to show evidence of discrimination in job hiring (GEMM Project, 2019). Why? Certainly, the link between social prejudices and educational levels is complex rather than straightforward, but this is insufficient to explain the persistence of discrimination.

In the case of more skilled jobs, one obvious explanation is that it is another consequence of the "pursuit of the best" under conditions where information about possible future performance in a job is especially incomplete. Here there is an important difference with the hiring of players by NFL teams. None of them can afford to take into account anything other than information directly relevant to *individual* candidates, because there is so much of it, which is one reason such a high proportion of its players are now non-white. (Since at least the early 1990s, overall the variation in earnings between white and black players has also been small; Kahn, 1992.) For most other jobs, the availability of necessary information is limited and often there is no supposedly identifiable and indisputable "best" candidate. Formal evidence about individuals' suitability has to be supplemented. Just as employment practices until the mid-20th century hinged on knowledge supplied by personal contacts, so there is still a role in decision-making for using knowledge other than that bearing solely on individuals themselves.

When there appears to be little to separate candidates, the "safest" best choice can be understood as one with *background experience* similar to those who frequently have proved "safe" appointments of this kind in the past. With an information deficit, assumptions about the traditionally "safest'" backgrounds (including, especially, earlier institutional affiliations) can be used alongside the goal of appointing the "best". That is why more attention is paid to prestigious institutions and proportionately more people are recruited from them, a point noted in the last chapter (Rivera, 2011). The larger the number of appointments being made, presumably in firms with more employees, the more that their recruiters will perceive that the need for considering "safety" is reduced or even eliminated.

It is, therefore, the relative lack of comparative information about individuals, which would otherwise have been decisive in hiring decisions about particular candidates, that results in applicants from racial minorities still being under-represented in many careers, though certainly not all. When they are insufficiently well represented in the historically "safest" pools of appointees, disproportionately they will not be hired now. One consequence is that among individuals with similar educational qualifications there will be divergence in the kind of careers open to them. In turn this will facilitate the "ethnic penalty" in pay mentioned in Chapter 3. This is not discrimination directed at the individual, but discrimination that arises from the inadequacy of comparative information, alongside the perceived utility of background information when hiring. Undoubtedly, many of those engaged in recruitment may not see or understand the logic of their own behaviour which, while clearly rational in its own way, is discriminatory. Consequently, they are less likely to recognize that its unintended consequences can indeed entail discrimination.

It is one of several ways in which the supplanting of proficiency at a skill by forms of positional competition fails to move recruitment towards a fully merit-based system. It is a goal that its own logic makes unachievable in the absence of levels of information that are rarely close to being attainable. However, beliefs that they could be then shape how the problem of unequal treatment in labour markets is understood. One result is that biases within these processes are not addressed effectively. Unfortunately, there is no quick fix for this. Typically, in contemporary labour markets the combination of an information deficit and the incentive for recruiters to do the "best" that they can for their employers partly reinforces the status quo. This is to the continuing disadvantage of those whose predecessors were shut out by overt prejudice.

Notes

1 One qualification to this argument is that in the past there was some discrimination in employing black players to the position that requires the most leadership skills on a team – quarterback.
2 The exceptions are the teams' two kicking specialists, some of whom are former soccer players.
3 Unlike cricket's Indian Premier League there is not an auction of players, with the teams bidding for services of specific players.
4 http://uk.businessinsider.com/nfl-draft-contract-values-2017-4. Accessed 22 February 2018.
5 As Brian Barry noted decades ago, luck can be conceived as the opposite of power: "If an individual's power is defined as his ability to change outcomes from what they would otherwise have been in the direction he desires, the likelihood of outcomes corresponding to his desires does not depend solely on his power. In addition … it depends on what the outcome would have been in the absence of his intervention. This is what I shall call luck" (Barry, 1980, p. 184).
6 In 2017 the European Court of Justice ruled that Uber was a transport company and not a digital service; http://www.bbc.co.uk/news/business-42423627.
7 See also Frank and Cook (1995).

References

Arthur, Rob and Binney, Zach (2016). *It's Hard to Tell How Good NFL Teams Are at the Draft*. Available at https://fivethirtyeight.com/features/its-hard-to-tell-how-good-nfl-teams-are-at-the-draft/. Accessed 9 February 2018.

Barry, Brian (1980). "Is it Better to be Powerful or Lucky?: Part 1", *Political Studies*, 28(2), pp. 183–194.

Ford, Robert (2008). "Is Racial Prejudice Declining in Britain?", *British Journal of Sociology*, 59(4), pp. 609–636.

Frank, Robert H. and Cook, Philip (1995). *The Winner-Take-All Society*. New York, NY: Free Press.

Frank, Robert H. (2016). *Success and Luck: Good Fortune and the Myth of Meritocracy*. Princeton, NJ and London: Princeton University Press.

GEMM Project (2019). *Are Employers in Britain Discriminating against Ethnic Minorities*. Oxford: Centre for Social Investigation.

Kahn, Lawrence M. (1992). "The Effects of Race on Professional Football Players' Compensation". *Industrial and Labor Relations Review*, 45(2), pp. 295–310.
O'Donnell, A. T. (1989). "The Neutrality of the Market", in Goodin, Robert and Reeve, Andrew (eds.), *Liberal Neutrality*. London: Routledge, pp. 39–60.
OECD (2015). "The Labour Share in G20 Economies", *Report Prepared for the G20 Employment Working Group Antalya*, Turkey, 26–27 February.
Palfreyman, David and Temple, Paul (2017). *Universities and Colleges: A Very Short Introduction*. Oxford: Oxford University Press.
Peter, Lawrence J. and Hull, Raymond (1969). *The Peter Principle: Why Things Always Go Wrong*. New York, NY: William Morrow.
Rivera, Lauren A. (2011). "Ivies, Extracurriculars, and Exclusion: Elite Employers' Use of Educational credentials", *Research in Social Stratification and Mobility*, 29(1), pp. 71–90.
Thelen, Kathleen (2004). *How Institutions Evolve: The Political Economy of Skills in Germany, Britain, the United States, and Japan*. Cambridge: Cambridge University Press.
Toynbee, Polly and Walker, David (2008). *Unjust Rewards: Exposing Greed and Inequality in Britain Today*. London: Granta.
WesternChief (2015). *What the Stats Tell Us About Drafting Positions by Round*. Available at https://www.arrowheadpride.com/2015/2/20/8072877/what-the-statistics-tell-us-about-the-draft-by-round. Accessed 9 February 2018.

5

GENERATIONS AND POLICIES

Accumulated wealth can be used in various ways to bolster the income and other resources of subsequent generations. In theory, the main instruments for restricting the perpetuation of unequal distributions of wealth over time are inheritance and gift taxes. In practice, they have been less radical than they might appear, partly because their role in raising substantial tax revenue usually has priority over egalitarian goals. The affluent typically make extensive use of financial planning to minimize wealth reduction for later generations of their own families. More recently, more modest middle-class households have benefitted from changes in British death duty that provide greater tax exemptions for family homes. Those who are not homeowners, mostly the least well off, have no such corresponding benefit. Since, for many, house ownership has become the principal form of investment for the former, a further inequality primarily along class lines has been introduced.

In this century, however, several controversial public debates have developed that do not relate directly to the overall distribution of resources between the main social groups. Instead, issues of inequality have emerged over the unequal availability of specific goods or services to successive generations, with often the most vocal dissatisfaction being expressed by the middle class, and not the poor. Housing, education and pensions are among the most frequent subjects of dissatisfaction, although in some sense, it is financial inequality that ultimately underpins the problems of unfairness they expose. Caution is required, though, when comparing distributions of goods over time, and one aspect of the private housing controversy illuminates this.

In 2017 a *Guardian* sub-heading for its coverage of a Resolution Foundation report read as follows: "David Willetts warns of 'housing catastrophe' as he launches study that lays bare intergenerational inequality" (20 September 2017). The ensuing article's discussion of that report (Corlett and Judge, 2017) then began as follows:

> Millennials are spending three times more of their income on housing than their grandparents yet are often living in worse accommodation, says a study launched by former Conservative minister David Willetts that warns of a "housing catastrophe" .... The generation currently aged 18–36 are typically spending over a third of their post-tax income on rent or about 12% on mortgages, compared with 5%–10% of income spent by their grandparents in the 1960s and 1970s ....

The newspaper implied that the report provided evidence of inter-generational inequality and unfairness. There are indeed both, although not between the two generations mentioned by the *Guardian*. Its article did not identify the evidence necessary for demonstrating a supposed *inequality*, as opposed to a *difference* between the "grandparents'" and the Millennials' situations. It failed to acknowledge that GNP per capita had increased by about 300 per cent (in real terms) since the 1960s. Suppose, post-tax, a contemporary family earns 100 units, of which it pays 33 for housing, while a 1960s family would have earned 33 units and spent perhaps 4 on its housing. The 2018 family still has 67 units left for other expenditures, while their counterparts had a mere 29 to spend. There is a massive difference between the two eras, but to invoke the notion of inequality in housing alone is inappropriate and misleading. The proportion of someone's resources spent on housing cannot be considered separately from the context of the overall level of resources available. Where generations are more alike in their resources, there is, indeed, some point to these sorts of comparisons. That is why the claim that a first-time purchaser in the current housing market today is disadvantaged by comparison with someone in 2000 does carry considerable weight. The large rise in house prices since then, accompanied by much more modest increases in real personal income, can be described in terms of inequality, and arguably unfairness, between one generation and the next.

This is not the only aspect of housing that is relevant to discussions of inter-generational inequality. With an ageing population, typically those who had relatives with sufficient resources to leave them an inheritance are now 61 when they receive it (Gardner, 2017). While such legacies may help these middle-class people to have a more comfortable old age, for most 61-year-olds it is much too late to benefit from an initial entry into the housing market. Arguably their own children might conceivably be more appropriate beneficiaries of the proceeds of a will. In terms of inter-generational inequality, how should we judge the reasonable claim of parents to have more comfortable later years versus that of the children to have earlier, and hence more valuable, access to the housing market?

The title of a book by David Willetts (2010) holds the generation that bought houses between the 1960s and the 1990s as somehow responsible for unequal treatment of later generations. Not only are simplistic inter-generational comparisons such as his misleading, but they direct attention away from the real cause of the legitimate complaints of those subsequent generations. Most certainly, there is culpability, but it rests far more with those who initiated and implemented public policies, including on housing, several decades ago. Their earlier actions helped put both renters and would-be homeowners of the 21st century at a relative disadvantage in getting what they wanted. Similarly, students today and future pensioners have been adversely affected by decisions taken many years previously. All three policy areas involve either a failure by governments or the limitations of markets in providing needed goods.

Housing

After 1945 Britain faced a major housing shortage, arising partly from wartime bomb damage but also because of persisting slum conditions in many inner-city areas. (As late as the 1960s some urban terraces still had earthen floors at ground level.) However, between 1951 and the late 1970s there was a massive expansion in the housing stock. Except for a couple of years in the late 1950s, and again briefly in the mid-1970s, the number of new housing units completed each year exceeded 300,000 and once, in the mid-1960s, completions totalled more than 400,000. While residents, especially in some new inner-city tower blocks, would rightly complain about the quality of their buildings, the earlier housing crisis had been resolved.

At the outset of the 1950s austerity regulations had restricted private sector builds, but after 1951 the incoming Conservative government eliminated them, and by the end of that decade this sector was completing more properties than the public sector. Although the latter would never again exceed the completions of the former, until the end of the 1970s it would always account for at least 40 per cent of completions. This was a stable model of provision, with private builds supplying the growing demand for home ownership and those by local governments providing most of the buildings needed for rental. Britain's rental market had changed significantly since the end of the 19th century. Earlier many middle-class families still rented accommodation, as did nearly all the working class, with rentals to both mainly having been supplied by private landlords. By the 1970s the rental sector was primarily in the hands of local authorities, and renters were predominantly working class.

On its election in 1979 the Thatcher government inherited a situation in which house builds had already been declining since the middle of that decade owing to the weakness of the national economy. Yet its approach would ensure that there was a permanent decline in public sector housing, so that by the beginning of the 1990s hardly any housing was being constructed by local authorities. Although properties built by registered social landlords – housing associations and so on – did increase, this growth was slow, and even this century they are completing fewer than 30,000 units a year.

The Thatcher administration's policy was driven by two related political considerations. One was to reduce public expenditure overall. Minimizing local authority capital expenditures by eliminating council housing builds would help facilitate that. The other was to weaken Labour party voting strength by decreasing the number of council tenants, the majority of whom were Labour voters. Most famously, there was a policy of allowing tenants to buy from their local council the houses they occupied. In fact, many of those who bought them had been Conservative voters previously, so that the policy prompted less vote switching among these new homeowners than was widely imagined at the time (Heath, 1991, p. 128). The principal thrust of the policy, though, was to eliminate the *building* of public housing, and this is the real origin of the present discontent about housing.

Underpinning the government's approach was a belief that the private sector could respond to demand for new housing under virtually any circumstances. It thereby committed a major error. In the absence of public sector housing construction the overall supply of housing had become relatively inelastic. High demand would not be met by much increased supply. Only briefly in the 1960s had new private completions exceeded 200,000 annually, and in the 30 years subsequently it reached that level just once. Even a medieval peasant could have explained why there would be such a problem. When a product is in extremely short supply, there is an increased incentive not to bring it to the market now, because the price may be higher still later. When only low costs are entailed by a delayed sale, greater profits can ensue. That was why, after harvest failures in the medieval era, those who owned grain might continue to store their supplies rather than respond to demand from peasants anxious to eat.

With late 20th century housing, several factors restricted the market response to rising demand. Most obviously, there was a shortage of building land in those areas of the country, notably in southeast England, where demand was strongest. Compared with many other advanced economies land prices were already high, thereby creating expectations of further rises. When landowners did sell, property developers could still have an incentive to delay building, or, especially in the case of completed tower blocks, neither sell nor rent them immediately in the expectation of higher returns from sales later. Although, from the 1950s, there were some years when house prices had declined, in the medium-to-long term they rose, often outperforming other possible sources of investment. This affected decisions about when to build and sell new housing. Furthermore, the growth of an international housing market tended to generate greater profits in building units in the London area for the rich worldwide rather than for middle-income Britons.

Nevertheless, there were also other causes of a modest private sector response. The 1947 Town and Country Planning Act had made provision for local authorities to create "green belts" around towns, and in 1955 the then Conservative housing minister adopted a policy of encouraging them to do so. Inevitably, despite its obvious benefits, this policy restricted the acreage potentially available for housing. When land could be purchased for either commercial or residential purposes, the former was often more profitable. Furthermore, until the late 1990s private building was primarily for owner occupation, and, during a recession, defaults on mortgages tended to reduce prices and further weaken the incentive to build immediately. Although the Housing Act of 1988 did increase the incentive for building buy-to-let properties, by providing guarantees to landlords on letting property to a tenant for a fixed period only, growth in overall housing supply was sluggish.

When demand for housing increased, as it did this century, the limitations of the Thatcher era policies became apparent. There was no longer a public housing sector that, together with the private one, could increase new housing stock to the levels required. Obviously, a critic of this analysis might plausibly argue that, as with most policies, housing was adversely affected by developments that might not have been predictable, all of which would fuel demand. Indeed this is arguably true of the continuing growth of one-parent families, of a cultural change towards greater autonomy for individuals in their living space, and of the massive growth in demand for modern housing by a vastly increased student population. Previously, as parodied in the comedy programme *The Young Ones* (first televised 1982–1984), students had often lived in the cheapest and least desirable housing. Within two decades that market was transformed in both the size and the quality demanded.

Even in the absence of these developments, however, housing supply after 1979 was always a disaster waiting to happen for some future generation. That danger increased from 1990, when a required U turn in policy should have been evident to any government. Longevity for women had been rising steadily since the 1930s, and after 1970 the expected life span for men also increased, and it did so sharply. An ageing population would restrict the supply of available housing on the market – both in the rental and in the homeowner sectors. It was the latter that would receive the greater media coverage, once it became clear that the problem was not a cyclical one correctable in the medium term.

A policy of continuing to subsidize home ownership, with tax relief allowance on mortgage interest payments being increased in 1983 and not abolished until 2000, predictably fuelled demand. Since property values were continuing to rise in the long term, this consolidated the widespread perception of home ownership as the most valuable investment open to a majority of the population. It supplemented the other main attractions of owner occupation: seeming security of tenure and the opportunity to alter the internal structure of one's accommodation to meet one's needs and tastes. However, owner occupation has disadvantages compared with renting: it is less flexible, and more expensive when changed personal circumstances require different accommodation. Furthermore, a rental sector should be providing a competitive alternative to ownership, one that is much cheaper because the renter does not have to pay interest on a mortgage, as a purchaser does, to cover eventually the capital borrowed. For a rental market to play that role, though, the overall supply of housing must be sufficient. If it is not, the cost of renting comes closer to that of ownership, so it becomes not a competitor to the latter but second best to it. In the long term what had been required in Britain were policies to counter a bias in favour of ownership, by increasing radically the supply of newly built accommodation for a rental market, thereby making renting a more attractive alternative for some in relation to ownership.

The need for more rental housing was finally recognized in the autumn of 2018 when the Conservative government announced that it would lift the cap on local authorities borrowing for the purposes of new building. Yet the number of units that might be built each year, perhaps 20,000, is a fraction of what was achieved under Conservative and Labour governments between the early 1950s and the 1970s. Even when the newly announced policy is enacted it will take years before the housing shortage is relieved, whereas in those earlier decades this could happen much more quickly.

The British situation was unlike Germany's, where post-war reconstruction had produced a proportionately larger rental sector. Under such conditions the two kinds of markets offer different advantages – and hence choice. Britain's housing shortage reduced the gap in overall short-term costs involved in rental and ownership, and at the same time provided an excellent investment opportunity for those who could raise the capital for the deposit on a mortgage. Thus, Britain has two tiers of housing, the lower one being for the less well off or for shorter term occupancy.

A shift in the balance between property ownership and renting could have been viable, but only with major state-led initiatives to help generate a long-term rental market. By dismantling local governments in the 1980s, and especially their role in housing provision, the Thatcher and later Major governments created conditions for a housing shortage. Between 2003 and the 2010s the proportion of Britons who were owner occupiers declined – from 71 per cent of the total to 64 per cent, the lowest level of ownership since 1986 (Resolution Foundation, 2016). This left successors to the two governments unable to counteract the eventual backlash from those who might wait years to buy their own accommodation.

As usual, the most vocally aggrieved are not the most impoverished, but those who had greater expectations than the reality confronting them. These are primarily young, middle-class, middle-income people whose options in housing are fewer than those open to their predecessors before 2000. Whereas in 1995–1996, 65 per cent of those between the ages of 25 and 34 and with incomes in the middle 20 per cent of their age group owned their own homes, only 27 per cent of their counterparts did so 20 years later (Cribb, Hood, and Hoyle, 2018). In real terms, the average cost of housing rose from £81,000 in 1977 to £137,000 in 1997, and then to £228,000 by 2017; that is, by 69 per cent in the first period and by 60 per cent from 1997 to 2017. But, while median household income had itself increased by about 60 per cent during the first period, it rose by a mere 35 per cent subsequently. Having to reduce one's expectations is a powerful driver of demands for political action.

The adult poor, who are disproportionately those who were born into impoverished families, are in a different situation. They still experience the lowest quality of housing, but for them this is nothing new, and they have fewer social resources than the frustrated middle class with which to generate sustained public protest.

Once consolidated, social protest can then snowball when there is more than one factor – such as housing – prompting discontent within the same or closely linked social groups. By the second decade of the 21st century there was another area of discontent with public policy among those who saw themselves worse off than their predecessors. This was post-secondary education, where once again it was not the most impoverished at the forefront of disaffection. Rather, it was children from less affluent middle-class families who now were in a position to enter higher education, but who would face much increased expense in doing so. Although some children from poorer families have the qualifications required for entry, proportionately they are a much smaller group within their class than these middle-class counterparts.

Education

With education, the most publicly displayed inter-generational discontent about unequal treatment was generated by much increased university tuition fees, as well as the accompanying high rate of interest payable on student loans, compared with a few years earlier. Before 1998 university tuition was provided free of charge to the student, and until 1999–2000 a system of student maintenance grants was still in place, although the value of those grants was considerably lower than immediately following their introduction in the 1960s. Loans replaced grants. Initially the tuition fee was set at £1000 annually, but by 2012 the maximum fee was now £9000. Student loans today attract interest at a rate above the retail price index. From one perspective, it is obvious that this seems to represent a major shift in the treatment of age cohorts separated by less than 20 years. Like housing, the contemporary controversy is a consequence of changes initiated in public policy decades ago, and it is an instance of earlier failure to provide equal treatment for all future generations. At its core is a long-term reshaping of public policy that is much broader than the issue of who pays for what.

In the 1960s education and training after secondary schooling were organized on two wholly different bases. A relatively small minority of adolescents, those moving on to either university or a teacher training college, had their fees paid for by their local governments and they also received a maintenance grant. While legally independent, the institutions in which they studied were mainly funded – through grants and fee payments – by central and local governments. Maintenance grants were means tested, thereby equalizing the burden.

The cost to the students and their families was relatively low, and the same was broadly true of those who left school and entered training for skilled jobs in industry, commerce and most professions. Typically, they were apprenticed to a firm, which paid them a small wage and often paid the fees for courses relevant to their "trade" provided by local technical, or other, colleges. The main "cost" to the trainee was the earnings forgone in not entering full-time employment on leaving school. However, once qualified, a former apprentice could expect to start earning more than those who were not qualified in any trade or profession. Between the mid-1960s and the early 1980s this training regime collapsed. The professions either downgraded direct entry from school or abandoned it entirely. (As noted in Chapter 2, some occupations like pharmacy wanted graduate entry because of both the status that it appeared to offer and the prospects of higher rewards it was assumed would ensue.) More serious, arguably, was the huge reduction in the number of apprenticeships in industry. Old skills became redundant, and training for most new ones was not undertaken under the old apprenticeship model. At the same time relevant public policy in Britain was starting to move in a wholly different direction, one that would change once again later – with disastrous results for social contentment.

Polytechnics, first proposed by the Labour government in 1965, were supposed then to form one-half of a new binary system in post-secondary education. This new element would parallel the universities, rather than being linked to them. Labour's minister of education, Anthony Crosland, argued that "increasing need for vocational, professional, and industrial based courses could not be met by the universities" and that "Britain could not stand up to foreign competition by downgrading the non-professional and technical sector" (Pratt, 1997, p. 8). The polytechnics would engage in work that was the *equivalent* of degree level work but would be of a *distinctive* kind. They would also provide other training and education at lower levels, together with sandwich courses (in conjunction with industrial partners) and part-time education. Because polytechnics would likely have more direct links with future employers, managing the flow of their "graduates" into specific sectors of the labour market might have been possible. It depended on the polytechnic sector being entirely separate from, but of equal status with, the universities. This binary arrangement was supposed to partly supersede the old apprenticeship system, by providing for more advanced training and education in skills following a secondary education.

During the 1970s the original objective of a technological sector being the equal of the university sector receded rapidly. The funding cuts required by successive economic crises that decade led to under-funding and pushed the polytechnics towards generating income in ways far removed from their original base in technology. The polytechnics' funding position had become "not so much 'different from, but equal to' the universities, as different and poorer" (Pratt, 1997, p. 239, citing Lewis, 1974). Too few would-be students were wanting to study their core subjects. Yet many who wanted courses in humanities or social science subjects were unable to obtain places at universities. The obvious solution for polytechnics was to open, and then subsequently expand, departments that had little or nothing to do with technology or industry. (Law and modern languages would be especially notable in flourishing there; Pratt, 1997, p. 111). Although there certainly were some polytechnic courses attracting high-flying school leavers unable to find suitable alternatives at a university, as well as those who valued innovations in course construction at the polytechnics, they were mainly receiving applications from those with lower qualifications than were universities.

By the early 1990s the situation was unsustainable. An obvious solution was to restructure the entire polytechnic sector, reducing it in size, but focussing on its original remit of more specific forms of training linked to technology. However, this would have been politically controversial and costly. Instead, the then Conservative government decided to turn the polytechnics into universities. Symbolically, when choosing their new names, all dropped the word "Polytechnic".[1] Discontent was merely postponed for two decades. Together with the decision of the subsequent Labour government in 1997–1998 to increase the number of full-time university students, the cost of this kind of education was becoming prohibitive for the British state. Because universities focussed primarily on academic study, firms were now little involved, even indirectly, in financing many aspects of post-secondary education or training, and they had relatively little incentive to do so. Yet, if the state could no longer payroll universities without increasing taxation, then only two strategies were open; both were adopted. One was to push the universities into becoming businesses, generating income from a variety of sources – including more graduate courses, more foreign students, and so on. Each now had an incentive to lower academic standards so that prospective applicants could be reassured that they could expect to receive a supposedly "good" degree there. The debasement of the credentials' "currency", discussed earlier, had begun. The other strategy was to make students pay for the cost of their higher education. A crucial weakness of this second strategy was that, for a large minority of the now increased numbers of university graduates, a degree was proving a poor financial investment.

As noted in Chapter 2, throughout this century nearly one-third or more of employed graduates who have been out of full-time education for 5 years have been hired in non-graduate roles (Office of National Statistics, 2013, p. 14).[2] Even in the best year for these graduates (2002), 28 per cent of them were not doing jobs of a kind for which a degree was, at least in theory, needed. They had graduated in 1997, a year with a booming economy. Obviously, economic conditions after the 2008 financial crisis had a further impact on the fit between university qualifications and jobs, especially for those just leaving university. In 2013, with an unemployment rate of 7 per cent, only 53 per cent of recent graduates were in graduate-entry jobs, compared with 63 per cent when the unemployment rate had been 2 per cent. However, the more important point is just how few of the supposed young elite – graduates whose undergraduate studies had been completed 5 years earlier – had been outside the graduate labour market when the national economy was strong. There remain too many graduates in the labour market, and more recent graduates are now paying far more to be in that situation. Mass student demonstrations ensued after 2010, when higher tuition fees were proposed and subsequently introduced, and they would be an important factor in contributing to the electoral collapse in 2015 of the junior partner in the coalition government (Cutts and Russell, 2015).

Several factors were responsible for this clear inequality between generations. The assumption made in the 1990s, that the growth in the graduate population would be no higher than the increase in the skilled jobs that could be done well only by graduates, was unsupported by relevant evidence available at the time. It proved to be false. The simultaneous policy of turning universities into semi-businesses created the worst of both worlds. Had each university been entirely free to set its own fee level, a tendency for all to charge near the maximum price, so as to be perceived as "serious institutions", would have been prevented. The fear that inegalitarian consequences would follow in the absence of a ceiling on fee levels would not have been realized, if at the same time the universities were required to link the fee payable by a student directly to parental income. That egalitarian principle was scarcely innovatory in the university sector. It had been used by the Conservative government in 1962 when mandatory maintenance grants were introduced.

Moreover, there was an information deficit. Had universities been mandated to collect and publish detailed information about the incomes earned by its graduates 5 years after graduation, and all graduates been required to supply it, these data would have provided information to applicants about their likely employment prospects.[3] Instead, the older truth, that a degree from one university would be worth much the same in the labour market as a degree from another, was allowed to perpetuate in circumstances when it was no longer true. Finally, university education is expensive to provide, and wasteful of resources when the skills supposedly being taught by institutions could be supplied by ones not having research as part of their remit. Rather than separating the traditionally linked functions of universities (research and teaching) into different institutions, the massive expansion of the university sector after 1992 perpetuated it. Many contemporary students are paying the unnecessary cost of attending institutions that are expensive to run.

The result was that during the 1990s successive governments built on policy mistakes made earlier to create generations of young people who are worse off than their near predecessors. They failed to consider alternatives that might in the short term have been more expensive, and more politically controversial, but which in the longer term would have provided greater protection to those finishing secondary education. Political short-termism triumphed over fairness.

Pensions

As with housing, inter-generational inequality in pension provision has arisen within a "mixed economy" of provision, although with an important difference in the relationship between public and private in the two policy sectors. After the National Insurance Act of 1946, the United Kingdom had a universal pension scheme, payable on reaching retirement age. It was based on fixed contributions made through compulsory National Insurance deductions from those in employment. Only people who had contributed for a minimum number of years would receive a full pension, and it was the same for all. The original purpose was to restrict mass impoverishment, but even on a full pension older people could have insufficient income to maintain a healthy life. Some would be eligible, therefore, and then receive Supplementary Benefits (before 1988) and later Income Support payments. This limitation of state pension provision resulted in successive state schemes for additional pensions intended to take more people away from a level barely above subsistence. (After 1978 there was SERPS, and then the Additional State Pension in 2002, followed by a new State Pension in 2016.[4]) While most retirees had the same potential entitlements from the state, they differed in their access to private pensions via an employer. In 2015 those in employment and paying into an occupational pension accounted for about half of all full-time workers, and about one-third of all employees.

The number of working people who were in occupational pension schemes had been relatively small in the 1940s and 1950s, with a majority of them being in the public sector. (It had been a benefit traditionally linked to that form of employment.) In the private sector employers had two incentives to introduce pension schemes. In an era when it was more common for an employee to stay many years with one firm, it provided an additional incentive for them to remain there. Pensions were not usually transferable between different employers. Reduced employee turnover, and its various associated costs, benefitted a firm. Moreover, with many people not living much more than 5 years beyond retirement, and especially men, it was relatively cheap to provide. For several reasons the situation changed radically in the 1990s, with five separate factors contributing to it.

There had been two decades of enhanced longevity among men, as well as a continuation of the earlier trend among women. Thus, while in 1987 there were 6 million people in receipt of occupational pensions, with just over one-half being former public-sector workers, by 1995 there were 8.5 million such pensioners and 59 per cent of them were now in the private sector. Payments were costing pension schemes much more than previously, while for employers they had become a less valuable incentive when hiring. Long-term service by employees with a single employer had become less common and was increasingly seen as incompatible with career progression. Non-transferability of pensions between firms reduced their role in recruitment under these changed conditions. At the same time, the move away from localized economies in Britain heightened competition between commercial firms, and thus enhanced the incentive to reduce employment costs. The financial value to a firm of a pension scheme was difficult to calculate, and therefore an obvious candidate for restricting future cost growth. On the other side of the employment relationship, after the 1970s those with a clear stake in preserving pension entitlement, and especially the trade unions, were in a weakened position outside the public sector. This made it more difficult for them to prevent reductions in future pension entitlements. Finally, like nearly all organized interests, unions tend to prioritize the conditions of service facing their current members over those who might become members in the future. Thus, any attempts to protect subsequent pensions for the latter would typically lose out to the interest of current employees. The result was entirely predictable.

In many ways the key decade was the 1990s when increased longevity was becoming an issue, and at the same time the private pension sector behaved as if little was changing. Indeed, as late as 1997 the pension scheme for university staff (USS) was permitted to reduce employer contributions for a year because, allegedly, the scheme was so much in surplus. At last, at the end of 2002, an emerging crisis affecting pensions generally led to the establishment of a commission that reported in two stages – in 2004 and 2005. Its reports, known usually as the Turner Report, outlined major long-term reforms that produced a political consensus and were then enacted after the 2010 election (Clark, 2016, p. 4). The state's role in pension provision was revamped. In effect, employees would have to work longer in the future before securing a full pension, and those enrolled in the new state-sponsored workplace pension saving model would be in a Defined Contributions (DC) scheme.

At the same time the private sector had already started to close the most generous type of pension schemes, those offering so-called "defined benefits" (DB), pushing employees into cheaper ones. That move accelerated this century, with a large increase in the number of employees in the cheapest schemes of all – DC. Precise data on this is disputed, because of different ways in which specific schemes can be classified, but one estimate for 2014 was that those enjoying DB were receiving 15 per cent of their overall earnings from employers in the form of contributions to their schemes. Employees with DC were getting less than 3 per cent.[5] In effect, market forces have generated a massive inter-generational inequality. Nor is this inequality confined to the purely private firms. Within the quasi-public sector, pension entitlement has declined. For example, USS, the scheme for university teachers and administrators, has been downgraded on several occasions since 2011. Those fortunate enough to retire before then receive far higher pensions than, proportionately, those who are now in their 20s and 30s and paying into the scheme can expect on their retirement.

Intergenerational inequality in housing and in higher education was the direct product of government action or inaction. While with pensions the state does not bear quite the same overall responsibility, the case does expose a major limitation of reliance on markets. They can never respond effectively to the wants of future generations, because relatively few such individuals are now present in these markets or able to protest. However, unlike housing, there could not have been an effective state-based solution to counter this aspect of social inequality. So far none of the schemes to boost the basic state pension has proved that attractive, or especially generous. Moreover, consider what would have happened to a government which recognized that increased longevity required greater contributions from current workers to their pension schemes, to protect the interests of future employees. It would probably have been electoral suicide for them, because the beneficiaries would have been unrelated to those bearing the cost. (As Theresa May's proposal for social care capping at the outset of the 2017 general election revealed, most people will protect the future interests of themselves and their offspring at the expense of more general future benefit.) Many of those between about 65 and 80 years of age, and who had private pensions, are the beneficiaries of good luck, and realistically, in a democracy there is little that could have been done to redistribute fairly that particular slice of luck. While that is not true of all areas of social inequality, luck undoubtedly is important in explaining some inequalities.

One challenge for a democratic state is to minimize luck as a determinant of inter-generational differences and, where it can, to attempt to provide equal treatment for successive generations. The truly egalitarian state would be one that responds not merely to demands for greater equality among its current population but equally to the needs of people in the future as well. The obvious constraint on this happening is that those generations have little, or no, political clout now. Thus far, it is mainly with respect to the environment that the notion of inter-generational equality has entered the political agenda more fully. Arguably, its position there arises partly because some environmental changes are now understood as having cataclysmic effects on human beings, and partly because in some cases those effects could be felt by living descendants. That might "concentrate minds" in ways that equality between generations on issues like pensions does not. Until there is such "concentration", this aspect of equality will not be taken wholly seriously as a political value.

Notes

1 American counterparts, as with the Virginia Polytechnic Institute and State University, which is usually known as Virginia Tech, have been less reticent in using the word.
2 Of course, on graduation many former students take non-graduate roles on a temporary basis, with a view to entering graduate employment later. But after five continuous years outside of graduate employment, entry becomes more difficult and subsequent entry less likely.
3 A partial and linked fee rebate 5 years after graduation would have generated an incentive for graduates to comply.
4 Although usually known as SERPS, the scheme was formally called the State Earnings-Related Pension Scheme.)
5 http://uk.businessinsider.com/defined-benefit-pension-transfer-wealth-from-workers-to-companies-2016-8. Accessed 21 February 2018.

References

Clark, Gordon L. (2016). "Behaviour, Choice and British Pension Policy", in Fenger, Menno, Hudson, John, and Needham, Catherine (eds.), *Social Policy Review 28: Analysis and Debate in Social Policy 2016*. Bristol: Bristol University Press, pp. 3–22.

Corlett, Adam and Judge, Lindsay (2017). *Home Affront: Housing Across the Generations*. Resolution Foundation Report, 20 September.

Cribb, Jonathan, Hood, Andrew, and Hoyle, Jack (2018). *The Decline of Home Ownership Among Young Adults, Briefing Note BN224*. London: Institute for Fiscal Studies.

Cutts, David and Russell, Andrew (2015). "From Coalition to Catastrophe: The Electoral Meltdown of the Liberal Democrats", *Parliamentary Affairs*, 68(Issue Suppl. 1), pp. 70–87.

Gardner, Laura (2017) *The Million Dollar Be-Question: Inheritances, Gifts and their Implications for Generational Living Standards.* Resolution Foundation Report.

Heath, Anthony (1991). *Understanding Political Change: The British Voter, 1964–87.* Oxford: Pergamon.

Lewis, Pamela (1974). "Finance and the Fate of Polytechnics", in Burgess, Tyrell and Pratt, John (eds.), *Polytechnics: A Report.* London: Pitman, pp. 110–148.

Office of National Statistics (2013). *Full Report – Graduates in the UK Labour Market.* Available at https://www.ons.gov.uk/employmentandlabourmarket/peopleinwork/employmentandemployeetypes/articles/graduatesintheuklabourmarket/2013-11-19

Pratt, John (1997). *The Polytechnic Experiment, 1965–1992.* Milton Keynes: The Society for Research into Higher Education and the Open University Press.

Resolution Foundation (2016). "Home Ownership Struggle Hits Coronation Street", *Press Release*, 2 August.

Willetts, David (2010). *The Pinch: How the Baby Boomers Took Their Children's Future - And Why They Should Give It Back.* London: Atlantic Books.

6

SOCIAL INEQUALITY AND DIVERSITY

Because there was no other broadly based source of division in Britain, social class lay firmly at the centre of economic, social and political inequality. Northern Ireland was different, of course, and remains so. There the major generator of inequality was religion. Whether you were a Protestant or a Catholic had a massive impact on many aspects of your life. In some localities in Great Britain too, and especially in Glasgow and Liverpool, migration from Ireland had also reproduced discriminatory personal treatment as well as a different kind of basis for local politics. However, these were essentially local variations and, outside Northern Ireland, they constituted merely a footnote when discussing inequality in the United Kingdom. Britain was widely understood then as being an overwhelmingly secularizing (formerly Protestant) country. Its population's ancestors were of a white European background, and its social values were dominated by a consensus partly founded on inequality. This included widespread acceptance of an assumption that, in a variety of ways, men could rightly be treated as superior to women. Usually they were regarded as heads of households, where the "normal" household was seen as a heterosexual couple with a family. The periodic challenges by the majority, that is women, to their partially inferior status were often followed by the persistence of the older status quo. Furthermore, for the first half of the 20th century social minorities within the country who did not accept their inferior treatment or status were both insufficiently small and powerless to mount any significant movement for change.

Thus, debating social inequality in Britain at that time was indisputably about class: how it operated, what its consequences were and whether it was capable of being modified or reformed. Overall that situation would change slowly during the 20th century, although it did so more radically from the 1950s onwards. Several factors were responsible for the transformation, one that would result in recognition that the discussion of inequality in Britain could no longer be confined to the direct consequences of a hierarchy based on status and income. There are many elements to this shift in how British social inequality is perceived, becoming more complex in the process because it more obviously has a broader base now. The best starting point is to consider the greater diversity that first became evident to most Britons during a period of about 25 years after the Second World War.

Diversification and social inequality

To many the clearly visible aspect of this diversification was post-1945 immigration. For many centuries Britain had been a country which at various junctures had attracted migrants. As an island it had appeared both as a (possibly) safer haven for refugees than did other European countries and as one of the more advanced economies in which skilled workers could thrive. In the commercial and industrial eras, from French Huguenots in the late 17th century to Jews from Russia two centuries later, Britain could be an attractive destination when avoiding religious discrimination and persecution. What was different about the two decades immediately after 1945 was that the migrants were predominantly from the British Empire and had different skin colours and frequently different religions. They were readily identifiable as those subjects of an empire whose most recent rulers had been white Britons, an empire then beginning terminal decline. For some Britons the newcomers' position within British society was perceived as being low, facilitating the creation of hostile social attitudes to them. A mere 10 years would elapse from the docking of the Windrush, with its migrants from the Caribbean being welcomed for their addition to the country's labour supply, to the Notting Hill race riots of 1958.

The British state's earlier focus on a labour shortage gave way to concerns about the social effects of migrant populations being concentrated in particular areas of larger towns. The pressure on some social amenities – and how this was perceived and misperceived by some white residents – formed the basis of moves to restrict further migration. The Commonwealth Immigrants Act of 1962 was the first of several measures intended to much reduce future emigration from the former empire. While the most overt social prejudice did decline slowly over the decades, it persisted nonetheless because skin colour, and in some cases religion and modes of dress, made it easy to identify many descendants of the original migrants. This would facilitate a perpetuation of discrimination in the labour market, in housing and elsewhere. One aspect of a new social diversity would develop, therefore, because there were new Britons. Many were not treated on similar terms by longer established Britons, and with some not wanting to see them treated on such terms at all.

Another major element in the emergence of a recognizable transformation in British society was older in origin than this. Despite the publicity generated by suffragists in the decade before 1914, their movement had not propelled the disparate ideas of 19th century first-wave feminism into the British mainstream. The belief that the different and unequal treatment of women in many spheres of life was fundamentally unfair was held strongly by only a minority – predictably, nearly all women. Most, including some women, simply assumed that the contemporary division of social and economic roles by gender was some form of "natural order". That order would be challenged in both world wars, when the combatant countries could raise mass armies only by encouraging women to take on jobs previously the exclusive preserve of men. When, at the conclusion of the two conflicts, British women were required to leave the jobs to which the state had originally recruited them, older assumptions about specific roles for the sexes would come to be questioned more strongly. But until the latter 1960s there was a delay in these catalysts taking effect.

At the same time there was also a shift in social values, and especially among various social elites, away from traditional mores that had emphasized long-established roles based on gender and conservative sexual behaviour. The permeation of this to other sectors of British society, and how it affected behaviour, was nonetheless incomplete. Just how limited the change often had been in practice would not become fully apparent until well into the present century. There had developed a gap between values that appeared to have become widely accepted, and which it had been assumed would therefore be translated into behaviour, and their being ignored in practice. For example, while there was now a "consensus" that men and women should be paid the same amount for the same job, in the absence of public scrutiny, many employers still pay women less. While in professional tennis, an industry where prize money for tournaments is published, equal pay eventually became established, in the British Broadcasting Corporation (BBC), where the remuneration of individual broadcasters and commentators had been kept private, it is taking much longer.

As significant as this kind of partial transformation, relating primarily to power in social hierarchies and discrimination in economic opportunities and rewards, there was a second change. The *kind* of equality being demanded by some – or alternatively being resisted by others – now includes elements very different from those earlier generations would have understood as central to an egalitarian agenda. During the second half of the 20th century social diversity was generating demands for equal legal rights, equal treatment of individuals and equal respect, in addition to equal benefits in labour markets, equal access to good housing and equal pension provision.

This transformation in how social inequality was understood previously and is now being contested differently is well illustrated by a much-publicized legal decision in 2018, often called the "gay marriage wedding cake" case. (It was a case in which the Equality Commission for Northern Ireland had contributed significantly to the legal costs of those who were claiming they were victims of inequality of treatment by a commercial firm.) Attention to the decision in *Lee v. Ashers Baking Company* is often focussed on the UK Supreme Court ruling that the Belfast bakery run by evangelical Christians was not obliged to make a cake containing the message "support gay marriage" (Supreme Court, 2018). However, as significant as this was the court emphasizing that its ruling did not undermine the priority to be accorded to equality of treatment for all social groups. Indeed, its judgement stated that "it is deeply humiliating, and an affront to human dignity, to deny someone a service because of that person's race, gender, disability, sexual orientation or any of the other protected personal characteristics." However, it also noted:

> that is not what happened in this case and it does the project of equal treatment no favours to seek to extend it beyond its proper scope .... The bakers could not refuse to supply their goods because [the client] was a gay man or supported gay marriage, but that is quite different from obliging them to supply a cake iced with a message with which they profoundly disagreed.

In other words, the court rejected the would-be purchasers' claim that failure to take their order constituted unequal treatment. No one can be compelled to supply a message with which they disagree, but refusing to sell to a client because of their sexual orientation would be unequal treatment and hence unlawful. The demand for equality of respect and treatment has become a key element of a new egalitarianism in an overtly more diverse society.

Of course, issues of equal treatment had been the subject of legal disputes long before the latter 20th century. The change in recent decades is essentially one involving a relative shift in importance – away from aspects of inequality directly linked to social class. Pulzer's observation in 1967 (p. 98), that class was the basis of British party politics with all else being mere embellishment or detail, could have been applied similarly in earlier decades to public discussions about social inequality. In neither case would statements about "embellishment" and "detail" be true of the current era, although arguably it is even less true of party politics than of social inequality.

There is yet a further way in which the bases of arguments about social inequality have been transformed. Partly because of relatively low upward social mobility, the relevance of inequality to families decades ago was as much about the fate facing their own children as it was about their present impoverishment. Consequently, during that earlier period debates about social inequality tended not to focus so much on class as it affected *individuals*, but more its impact on a particular social unit – the supposed "traditional" *family*. As noted earlier, that unit was widely understood then as comprising a heterosexual couple with, typically, the man at its head. Other groupings of adults were perceived as less significant, because less numerous or less "respectable", than this. Inequality was largely conceived in one dimension: it was about a nation-wide class divide, in which on both sides of that divide a "traditional" family unit was the central social structure.

One-dimensional inequality

Ironically, in one respect this one-dimensional understanding of British inequality was already becoming anachronistic at the very time that class started to become fixed as the centrepiece of British politics, that is, immediately after the First World War. The industrial base of the British economy weakened from 1920, with at least one million people unemployed every year for nearly two decades. However, those families living in the more industrialized regions outside southern England were disproportionately its victims. Regional differences became further pronounced after the mid-1930s. Although the initial impact of the Great Depression had been national, diversity emerged still more strongly from the mid-1930s onwards. The south and the Midlands enjoyed major economic resurgence, while the traditional industrial regions in the rest of England, along with Scotland, Wales and Northern Ireland, did not. Although there had been hunger marches since the early 1920s, the very starting point of the Jarrow March (to London) in 1936 came to symbolize enduring regional differences in economic welfare. Social inequality now varied by area as well as along class lines.

Very little ensued, however. After 1945 the poorest regions continued to be those outside the south, but until the 1960s the post-war full-employment economy produced only limited public debates about development policies to counter regional inequalities. When they did commence, the policies of successive governments little altered the fundamental imbalance in the prosperity of the various regions. Indeed, with the growing relative importance of the financial sector, London and the southeast began to pull ahead of all others. During the present century there was not so much a country divided in prosperity along north–south lines, but one split between the London metropolitan area and most of the rest of the United Kingdom.

By then there had also evolved a fundamental change in how the scope of inequality was understood in political and policy-making domains. There were three intersecting strands to this transformation, which subsequently would further break down the old one dimensionality of how Britons understood their society's inequalities.

From utilitarianism to rights

The first strand lay in the elite world of academics, lawyers and public intellectuals. Its origins were as much in the United States as in Britain itself, and the debates began as early as the late 1950s. Discussing this in 1979, the most distinguished British legal philosopher of the 20th century observed that everyone familiar with writing in Britain and in America in the previous 10 years could not doubt that there had been a transition from an "old faith" to a "new faith". The "old faith" was a common belief in some form of utilitarianism. While there might be disagreements about how to base public policy on the different *interests* that people had, there had been agreement that interests should be the moral foundation for making public policy. When defending their own conception of the *public interest*, political parties would likely still be in conflict, but they were, nonetheless, contesting shared territory. By contrast, according to Hart (1979, p. 828), the "new faith is that the truth must lie not with a doctrine that takes the maximization of aggregate or average general welfare for its goal, but with a doctrine of basic human rights ...".

The application of the "new faith" embraced not just generalized or abstract rights, such as a right to family life, but also rights that applied to specific groups because their members might be vulnerable to unequal or unfair treatment by others. This focus on rights started to shift the grounds on which equality would be discussed and debated in public forums, a point that the judges' comments in the "gay marriage wedding cake" case illustrates. This focus is no more, but importantly also no less, supportive of egalitarianism than utilitarian forms of justification: they are egalitarian in different ways. The "new faith" is egalitarian because rights protect individuals either equally or with the aim of protecting the vulnerable from unequal treatment. All varieties of utilitarianism, however, treat the interests of each person as being equal, with justifiable public policy then being derived by adding those interests together in some way. This transition from interests to rights aided political movements, originating in various social groups and demanding equal treatment, that had found themselves on the wrong end of social distribution. They included different racial groups, women and, later, disabled people and also gay and lesbian groups and, most recently, transgender people. In varying degrees and in various ways all found themselves in some respects disadvantaged in access to employment, in education, by social exclusion and by unequal treatment.

Subsequently prominent public intellectuals engaged with this debate in numerous ways. For example, the American Elizabeth Anderson (1999) has argued that egalitarians should not focus on the distribution of divisible goods, in the way that most applications of what Hart called the "new faith" had. According to her and others, social justice should now be based on changing social norms rather than in redistributing resources. Whereas Hart was reporting on a development that *had* commenced within the previous two decades, Anderson was propounding an argument that inequality *should* be conceived in very different terms. However, she was writing in an era of relative economic prosperity, and depressed economic conditions after 2008 have altered that context. Thus, in Britain outside academia the influence of her kind of ideas has so far been limited, and debates about inequality generated by the role of diversity have continued to be dominated by issues relating to the distribution of various social resources.

Mobilizing for rights

Undoubtedly this shift in how some elites understood social inequality assisted groups in their lobbying for legislation, and their pressing for oversight agencies responsible for specific forms of denial of access, and so on. Nevertheless, success would also depend on mobilizing themselves politically. That usually required engaging with politics more broadly, and not just operating through the previous "usual channels" linked to political parties and well-established interest groups. In many ways the scale of the problems facing groups challenging inequality is best illustrated by the case of women, because they might be thought to have been better placed than others to effect change. Women had always formed more than half the population, unlike, for example, the transgender community which still constitutes only about 1 per cent; unlike racial minorities, most of their families had not been recent migrants to the country; unlike the gay community, they were not constrained before 1967 as having an illegal lifestyle; and unlike the disabled they were not widely identified as simply "unfortunate".

Moreover, they had not earlier been subject to special restrictions on *entry* into educational resources, the main route to upward social mobility. Under the 11+ regime of pre-1970s Britain, girls were not "second-class" children at secondary school level: proportionately more girls than boys entered grammar schools. In the early 1950s nearly 20 per cent of 13-year-old girls attended maintained and assisted Grammar Schools, compared with 19 per cent of boys. In Wales, with its much larger grammar school sector, the gap was even greater; 34 per cent of 13-year-old girls, but only 30 per cent of boys, had entered its grammar schools (Campbell, 1956, p. 39). Overall, they had outperformed boys in the 11+ examinations (Dempster, 1954, pp. 74–75). The problem facing girls was that cultural pressures, lack of job opportunities comparable to those for boys and other factors all made for an even higher incidence of early exit from grammar schools than that exhibited by boys at the time.[1]

Girls left school early because they had relatively little chance of entering the more interesting and better paid jobs. Various practices in recruitment and in promotion procedures ensured that their prospects were significantly worse than for boys and men. Consequently, despite the equal provision made for them on entry into grammar schools, few went on to university. Even by 1970–1971 only 29 per cent of full-time university students were women. For women who did not have these opportunities the situation was similar. In less skilled jobs they were frequently paid less than men for comparable work, just as women graduates usually were. This started to change from the later 1960s through various forms of political action. Second-wave feminism of that era also generated publicity for the inferior social roles to which women were usually consigned, as did industrial action and notably the strike for equal pay at Ford's Dagenham plant in 1968. The first significant result of this was the Equal Pay Act of 1970, which came into force in 1975. Political action and mobilizing thus forms a second strand in the transformation from a uni-dimensional understanding of social inequality to its being recognized as being more diverse in form.

Over the course of the next 25 years there was legislation to establish official agencies with responsibilities, albeit rather confined in scope, whose purpose was to help reduce the unequal treatment of different groups. The Sex Discrimination Act of 1975 established the Equal Opportunities Commission; the Race Relations Act of 1976 aimed to prevent discrimination on grounds of race and set up the Race Relations Commission, which was eventually followed by the Disability Discrimination Act of 1995 and then a Disability Rights Commission in 1999. With the Equality Acts of 2006 and 2010 all these agencies were then consolidated.

Of course, none of this meant that discrimination and unequal treatment were eliminated. They were reduced somewhat, and the forms that they took altered but, to take just one example, there continue to be far fewer women than men working in the upper echelons of Britain's financial sector. For jobs where the pay of individuals is discretionary, many women continue to earn less than male counterparts in jobs involving identical responsibilities. This occurs in public as well as private employment. One irony of the controversy over the salaries of BBC correspondents in 2018 was that 50 years earlier media coverage had been important for the Dagenham strikers in winning their equal pay dispute. The main result, therefore, of group action and state intervention over a period of four decades was that they legitimized claims to counteract unequal treatment of different groups, but without necessarily eliminating those practices. Furthermore, indirect discrimination, which involves a practice, procedure or rule that applies to all but has a specific negative impact on some, is usually more difficult to identify and remedy. Thus, inequality of treatment persisted, though it could no longer be dismissed summarily as irrelevant or merely an aspect of some imagined natural order.

Social change

The third strand of change was social. Not only was the class system altered – with a relatively much larger and more diverse middle class – but family structure was as well. The notion of a standard model of families, a heterosexual married couple with a few children, as the central unit around which discussion of social inequality had to revolve disappeared. Curiously perhaps, in practice the dominance of that model had been relatively recent. In Victorian Britain one-parent households were common because of the premature deaths of many adults. It was one of the main causes of impoverishment, especially when the male head of household, whose income could not be replaced, died. The early death of both parents was usually disastrous for their orphans. In addition, the household of a nuclear family was often supplemented then by elderly relatives lacking means of support, for whom the only alternative was destitution. Of course, Victorian middle-class Christian values had led to the veneration of the heterosexual married couple, but it was during the 20th century that this nuclear family model became more common. Improved health and greater workplace safety both made for more continuity in first marriages, while easier divorce did not become available until 1969. Thus, despite the carnage of the male population in the First World War, during the inter-war years a one-dimensional view of inequality, based on the supposed "traditional" family unit, could take hold. It would continue to shape mainstream public attitudes for nearly 50 years.

One aspect of its undermining was the collapse of the hegemony of Christian notions of what constituted a family, and of how a society should be organized. During the later 20th century unmarried couples were no longer seen as having given birth to a bastard, but as having chosen not to marry or not to live together permanently while raising a child. In the present century gay men and lesbians can now marry, adopt children, have a child via surrogacy and so on, all of which were impossible decades earlier. The notion of what it was for a unit to be a family expanded. One consequence was that more attention became focussed on the individual (rather than on a multi-person unit, the "traditional" family) when discussing aspects of inequality. With housing, many individuals now wanted to have their own accommodation rather than share it. This would have considerable impact on a growing demand for housing units. Until the 1960s a single person would most frequently rent a room in someone's house ("digs"), where that room would usually be their only private space and use of other parts of the house restricted. While communal living persisted, especially among the young in sharing flats, the demand for more autonomy in living arrangements altered patterns of habitation. The Housing Act of 1919, the legislative reality of Lloyd George's claim to provide "homes fit for heroes", had focussed on building houses for "traditional" families, and not on providing their own accommodation for individuals. A century later that kind of approach to social inequality would be dismissed as inadequate and insensitive. Individuals have come further towards the centre of public debate about some aspects of inequality than they were.

Equality: rights versus interests

The impact of these transformations has been that more social groups have sought, and sometimes acquired, rights that help protect them against unequal treatment. Even when these claimed rights have not been recognized in law, policies by public and private organizations have sometimes been changed. One instance illuminating the effect of a shift in public debate relates to transgender people, who were regarded as a completely marginal (and seemingly irrelevant) small minority until the end of the 20th century. A specific aspect of their changed status illustrates Hart's claim of a transition from an "old faith" to the "new faith" when a policy is being justified. This is whether transgender individuals should be able to choose between using either a public toilet designated for men or one for women. Typically, the "old faith" supported the notion that no one could exercise choice on the matter because to do so would make women more vulnerable to male pestering or assault in public toilets. The justification was that segregation provided women with some protection. A strict segregation policy hinged on a straightforward "public interest" defence: overall, the majority of the population has a higher level of physical safety, because that separation is relatively easy to enforce. All women are thereby potential beneficiaries. The "new faith" position is that the rights of a transgender person are infringed, if they are not allowed to choose the toilet facility in which they feel more at ease or are less likely to experience abuse from others. To deny them choice is to subject them to discrimination, as individuals. This is a different basis for equality, and it generates different consequences for public policy.

It does more than this, though. If increasingly the "currency" of contemporary political debate is rights, then women who wish to secure their personal safety now have a greater incentive to assert their claim in terms of their own rights being infringed. Rights are often understood as "trumping" other arguments; that is, that they have a special normative force.[2] To counter a claim based on rights, another right, one that is superior, has to be asserted. However, when rights claimed by different individuals or groups come into conflict with others, and one is not clearly superior to another, what is the basis for choosing between them? Whatever is decided, someone will have lost. While a fair process will have treated them equally, of course, the result will not leave them equally well off. Diversity has obvious advantages for a society, and some diversity is inevitable, but facilitating the promotion of equality in society by means that are consensual is not necessarily one of them. The rights of different groups can, and do, conflict, because only with some rights is there a strict hierarchy of them. Rights may be "trumps" but, unlike playing cards, the relative value of many of these "trumps" is not known and may vary in different contexts.[3] We do not know which "trump" might "overtrump" another. Asserting a right is not to play the equivalent of a winning card but is merely to provide another argument in your favour.

In politics, Hart's "old faith" had helped to obscure and diffuse conflicts of interest to some degree, and thereby over time it assisted in the process of partly reconciling them. Most certainly, it did not eliminate these conflicts, but it made the political management of them more feasible. The reason for this is that, when exercised well, it made it possible for the varying interests to believe that they had gained something from the particular phase of the process – although not obtaining everything they wanted. Although not generating long-term social consensus, it did tend to produce shorter term acquiescence. The appearance of the policy process was not inherently zero-sum in character. Reconciliation of conflicts over rights is typically more contentious, because adversaries frequently believe that the rights that they claim are in some sense absolute when they are not. Asserting claims on the basis of rights that are in conflict with someone else's rights tends to raise a sense of entitlement, when not all those who feel so entitled can then be satisfied. Thereby political management of social conflict becomes more complex.

The more diverse and fragmented the social groups whose interests are recognized as being subject to unequal treatment, the more difficult it may be in practice to facilitate the introduction of procedures that provide for equal, comparable treatment. The Paralympics and other disability sports illustrate this problem (Powis and Macbeth, 2019). With many disabilities, although unlike total blindness, for example, there are varying degrees to which individuals are disadvantaged in a sporting competition, because of the extent or scope of the disability an individual has. Some athletes benefit, and others lose out, depending on how the categories are delineated. Consequently, devising rules for different categories of competitor has arguably been the main issue confronting these sports since they first started to organize and then attract spectators. Establishing fair rules is complex and, worse, can facilitate cheating over classification in ways that can maximize one person's chances of success by their being placed in a category that puts most of their competitors there at a disadvantage. Typically procedures that would minimize cheating or unfairness in classification are far more expensive to operate than simpler ones which are less effective, so that disgruntlement follows when the former are unaffordable. Sometimes the practical pursuit of equality eliminates one inequality but creates others – quite possibly ones less comprehensive or pernicious, but still sources of unfairness.

The general point to be derived from this is the following. The more sub-categories of a group within a society accorded recognition as distinct, separate and meriting different rights or treatment, the more complex and potentially arbitrary become attempts to "level the playing field" overall. This is not an argument against making such attempts. Rather, it is to say that recognition of diversity tends to make the *application* of egalitarian ideals even less straightforward than under the one-dimensional notion of social inequality that once dominated Britain. Engaging with social inequality now is just more complicated than it was, and at the same time, and in many respects, inequality remains a central feature of British society.

Notes

1 In 1936–1937 early leaving among 14-year-olds accounted for 44 per cent of 14-year-old girls, but only 37 per cent of boys (Spens Report, 1938, pp. 100–101).
2 The most famous proponent of this notion was Ronald Dworkin (1984).
3 In addition to different rights conflicting, the assertion of rights for one group may result in those of another being overlooked. One instance of this point being made was in 2018 when a member of the House of Commons Select Committee on Women and Equalities claimed that an enquiry into transgender issues focussed on this group "obtaining legal recognition of their preferred gender and 'didn't really look at the implications for women as a whole. I think that was fundamentally flawed'"; https://www.theguardian.com/society/2018/oct/17/transgender-law-reform-has-overlooked-womens-rights-say-mps.

References

Anderson, Elizabeth S. (1999). "What is the Point of Equality?", *Ethics*, 109(2), pp. 287–337.

Campbell, Flann (1956). *Eleven Plus and All That: The Grammar School in a Changing Society*. London: Watts.

Dempster, J. J. B. (1954). *Selection for Secondary Education: A Survey*. London: Methuen.

Dworkin, Ronald (1984). "Rights as Trumps", in Waldron, Jeremy (ed.), *Theories of Rights*. Oxford: Oxford University Press, pp. 153–167.

Hart, Herbert (1979). "Between Utility and Rights", *Columbia Law Review*, 79(5), pp. 828–846.

Powis, Ben and Macbeth, Jessica Louise (2019). "We Know Who Is a Cheat and Who Is Not. But What Can You Do?: Athletes' Perspectives on Visually Impaired Sport", *International Review for the Sociology of Sport*. First published online 3 February.

Pulzer, Peter G. J. (1967). *Political Representation and Elections: Parties and Voting in Great Britain*. New York, NY: Praeger.

Spens Report (1938). *Report of the Consultative Committee on Secondary Education with Special Reference to Grammar Schools and Technical Schools*. London: HMSO.

Supreme Court (2018). *Case Details: Lee (Respondent) Versus Ashers Baking Company Limited and others (Appellants)(Northern Ireland)*. Available at https://www.supremecourt.uk/cases/uksc-2017-0020.html. Accessed 22 April 2019.

7

INEQUALITY IN A DEMOCRACY

There are many ways in which social and economic inequalities can affect the conduct of democratic politics. Indeed the whole notion of democracy presumes some degree of equality in a society. Obviously, how extensive the scope of that equality has to be depends initially on the meaning of the word "democracy". For some writers, including Jack Lively (1975), democracy was quite simply political equality, and therefore the idea of democracy should be examined on the basis of that. However, this approach just pushes the discussion on to the question of what is meant by "political equality" itself. Does it mean that every person or interest in the society has the same influence over government policies? Does it mean that every viewpoint should be heard publicly? Or is it just a shorthand for "one person, one vote" in an election? Or what? And there are many other issues that could be raised in this context. For our purposes two broad matters are particularly significant. To what extent are the resources needed to exercise influence in Britain's political system distributed unequally? Is every opinion in Britain heard on an equal basis, and does greater equality in this respect aid democratic rule or possibly harm it?

Money and political equality?

A crude summary of Victorian attitudes with regard to equality might proceed as follows. Many upper- and middle-class people feared any egalitarian attempts at redistributing economic resources because its radical aims would necessarily be at their expense. For the middle class, opposition to enlarging state activity to improve the condition of the poor was due partly to the tax burden already falling disproportionately on them, rather than on the landed classes. As a result, an expansion of the franchise to include at least some of the working class was always viewed with great suspicion by other classes. The sheer numerical superiority of the former class was expected to lead shortly after their enfranchisement to their using political power to redistribute wealth in various ways. Of course, while enfranchisement of part of the working class in the 1880s (some men) and full adult enfranchisement between 1918 and 1928 was accompanied in the mid-20th century by partial redistribution, it was not on the scale many feared earlier.

In the absence of an overthrow of the British political regime itself, "one person, one vote" would always have been required for enacting any radically egalitarian policy, but it would prove wholly insufficient for that purpose. As one leading European scholar noted in the mid-20th century: "Votes count in the choice of governing personnel but other resources decide the actual policies pursued by the authorities" (Rokkan, 1966, p. 106). The point is not just that elections do not decide directly the policies enacted by a new government, but that resources other than the vote partly determine who it is that becomes the governing personnel after an election and hence indirectly what they do. Consequently, votes count in elections but so too do other resources. When Rokkan was writing in the mid-1960s the United Kingdom was at the start of a major transition in the balance of those resources required for contesting elections.

The power of money in influencing election results had been reduced dramatically after 1883 when the Corrupt and Illegal Practices Prevention Act was enacted. Law now strictly controlled and limited how much could be spent in parliamentary elections, although some recent analyses have questioned whether the act had quite the striking effect earlier generations believed that it had had (Rix, 2008). Its focus was entirely on what could be spent within each constituency, and for decades it limited the role of money in election campaigns. It could do so because there was little national campaigning on which money could otherwise be expended. The resources that mattered most in those years were organizational: supporters active in constituencies and, after the formation of the Labour Party in 1900, those in trade unions. Although the combination of resources on which the different parties relied differed, until mid-century there was a rough balance overall between the major parties when campaigning. With the advent of national television and later with social media this situation would be transformed massively.

Neither money, national media, mass advertising nor any other resources determined directly which political parties controlled parliament, but indirectly they shaped what happened. This was not just during the campaign periods themselves, but in the months and years prior to an election. The voters whose votes were counted, therefore, were not operating in an environment where they were ever entirely free from the kinds of influences of those interests with access to greater resources. Overall just how inequalities in resources change how political issues are structured for the public, and over time how much they then affect who wins elections, is difficult to assess precisely. Some, including the prize-winning journalist Carole Cadwalladr, have argued that Facebook's influence today is so great that it undermines democracy itself (Cadwalladr, 2019). Drawing on subsequent evidence about the conduct of the 2016 Brexit referendum, she argues that hidden funding and false claims made in communications sent only to sympathetic voters on the internet were outside public scrutiny both at the time and later. Nevertheless, even those who might dispute her argument could not claim plausibly that resource inequalities lack impact on democratic outcomes. Yet assessing how political agendas were set in the long term is highly complex even for the era prior to that of the internet and the unregulated communication that it facilitated began.

Then and now financial inequalities in the conduct of democratic politics mattered. Indeed, there is compelling evidence from American politics that money really does count in shaping outcomes, and it counts more today than ever before (Page and Gilens, 2018, and Bartels, 2018). Although for various reasons it may count for somewhat less in British politics than in the United States, it is undoubtedly the case that political spending in Britain has increased greatly and, just as importantly, how it is sourced has become more fragmented and indirect. That makes keeping tabs on who is funding whom or what for more difficult. The Brexit referendum provided clear evidence of how multiple organizations may be involved in funding political causes and campaigns, and that "following the full money trail" entirely has become so complicated as to be virtually impossible. Consequently, the secrecy of the pre-1883 era has returned, at least in part. Unfortunately, how to counter the impact that money might have, so that there is greater equality in political debate and in electoral contests, produces suggested solutions but until now no major reform.

Nonetheless, reformers have to proceed with caution. As with reform in any field of activity, seemingly plausible changes often turn out to have unwanted consequences – either directly or indirectly. For example, attempts at restricting financial contributions to election campaigns or limiting campaign expenditures could end up substituting advantage to another set of groups in place of the ones for whom regulation was intended. During the 1990s, while looking back on the major reforms of US campaign finance in the 1970s, the late Nelson Polsby used to argue this point (Brady, Polsby, and Robinson, 1997). Rather than attempts at limiting private funding and spending in campaigns, which he argued were not fully effective, he believed that it was another reform of that era which had been especially significant. One of the leading authorities on the US Congress in the 20th century, Polsby emphasized the role of immediate public disclosure of all financial donations. So long as a free press and political oppositions could easily and quickly identify the original source of money, it became possible to counteract its effects during campaigning. For him, this was the stuff of democratic politics, and appropriate rules of disclosure were needed so that it could work effectively. This is broadly similar to the approach that Cadwalladr and others are promoting currently.

At least two problems, however, have become evident this century in both Britain and the United States in making this kind of solution work less well in the form in which it had been enacted in 1970s America. One is that "shell" organizations have been set up to circumvent the rules, so that establishing who the original backers and funders are takes time and may be difficult to establish ever. The other is the new ability for money to be moved rapidly from one legal entity to another, so that tracing the trail of money becomes sufficiently complex that it may not be completed until long after a campaign has ended – if then. Regulating political money so that its real sources can be exposed to the public quickly is no longer a matter that any single reform can hope to settle for decades afterwards, in the way that the British Act of 1883 did for campaign expenditures. Those who want to use money to influence politics will always try to find ways of circumventing existing regulations, and evasion is easier today. This means that regulation must be a continuous process if this form of political inequality is to be restricted. In its enactment, obviously, issues of privacy might be invoked in opposition to reform. However, there is an important difference between having a right to know how any individual or organization spends money privately or on directly commercial matters and expenditures in the political realm. Democratic politics is fundamentally a public activity, not an extension of private affairs. The practice of democracy requires appropriate rules of disclosure, precisely because they are not private; otherwise the underlying democratic principle of political equality can be undermined.

A new elite versus new radicals?

One consequence of the kind of increased political inequality that has developed in the past few decades has been the further weakening of the potential power of those demanding radical redistribution of economic resources, something so much feared by many affluent Victorians. This was especially true in the early and middle decades of her reign, but by the time of franchise reform in the 1880s it was political advantage that tended to drive conflict over the extension of the franchise. However, there were also other factors reducing the possible appeal of such an agenda – at least before the 2008 financial crisis and its aftermath. Even when it constituted a numerical majority of the population, the working class was not a cohesive group congregating around a single set of political ideas. In the early 1950s, at the height of class voting in Britain, only about two-thirds of that class voted for the party most supportive of some form of economic redistribution – the Labour Party. Changing class structure, with a relative decline in the size of the working class, further decreased that base of support.

It could be argued that there was now no new single source of inequality in British society which could replace the much-diluted class conflict at the centre of British politics. In recent years that assumption has been challenged. There are some who would argue that there is an emerging political division in Britain, one based on education – between those who have educational credentials, of at least undergraduate degree level, and those who do not. The main evidence for this claim comes primarily from perhaps the most striking feature of the Brexit referendum result of 2016. There was a strong relationship then between being more highly educated and voting to "Remain", while those with lower educational qualifications were predominantly voters for "Leave" (Goodwin and Heath, 2016). With the former group losing, Michael Young's imagined future in 1958, of a meritocratic elite being overthrown in Britain in 2033, might be understood as merely being overly cautious with respect to timing! Undoubtedly, the referendum result could be interpreted as the educated getting their comeuppance from those who had failed to be convinced of the benefits of close co-operation with other European countries. However, does this provide evidence of a new, longer term, cleavage in British society, one that will drive political behaviour from now on?

On one side, it can be argued that the protracted and increasingly bitter political conflicts accompanying the government's attempts to negotiate a deal with the European Union (EU) for exit revealed divisions in British society that before seemed not to be present. Because final agreement on any post-Brexit arrangements might take many years, it is certainly possible that the frustrations and anger that the Brexit referendum generated could be evident during that entire period. The long-term repercussions on how different groups align themselves politically in those years might conceivably be massive. Perhaps the more educated versus the less educated could dominate British politics into the future. There is, though, a counterargument to this.

The earnings of graduates are now far more diverse than they used to be, with a growing income gap between those with high qualifications and those with lesser ones (Naylor, Smith, and Telhaj, 2015, pp. 14–16). For graduates who do well out of the system of positional competition for educational credentials, the rewards are indeed high and far exceed the costs incurred in obtaining them. Yet, for others who are ill positioned after their studies to move into the highly skilled job market, the situation is very different; many are not obtaining what they thought they would (Ware, 2015a, 2015b). While present rules relating to loan repayments on fees might not impoverish some of them, because they will never earn enough in their lives to trigger much repayment, they will still have incurred costs in obtaining their degree. The interests of the two kinds of graduates differ sufficiently that theirs seems an unlikely long-term political alliance, especially after the extended Brexit and post-Brexit era.

Moreover, for some graduates during later employment, automation (including the expanded use of robots in product design and in organizing service provision) may limit not just the financial value of their investment in education, but also any significant use in employment of their acquired intellectual skills. Educated beyond their employers' needs, but having obtained skills through education, they might conceivably become the new Jacobins of politics, or at least form an element of the politically discontented. Of course, it could be argued that this suggestion merely parallels a similar, unfounded, fear of some Victorians. They worried about the consequences of educating the working class beyond a minimum standard, because it would provide them with tools of use in attempting to overthrow the social order. Although they were proved wrong, theirs was a society where the future would prove favourable: it would provide both subsequent long-term economic growth and slow, modest, social redistribution towards greater equality. These conditions are not present currently and might conceivably not be for much of this century. In a world lacking the social deference of the Victorian era, it is not evident why the divergent interests of different sectors of the graduate population would cohere into a political alliance when economic growth is relatively low and income inequality is not diminishing.

Unequal opinions

There is another important difference between the politics of equality today and that of Britain's democratic era earlier, which in this case is as recent as pre-1980. Demands are being contested in a political arena in which authoritative opinion counts for much less. The Victorian fear of the weight of numbers in elections was negated in part by the role played by "informed opinion". Those whose range of knowledge put them in a good position to separate plausible ideas from implausible ones were listened to, and their views accepted more widely than are their counterparts' today. This helped structure the nature of public debate. It did not prevent discussion of possible major changes in the distribution of social and economic resources, but it restricted the range of ideas and proposals that could be taken seriously by more than just a tiny minority.

Democracies always take pride in the diversity of opinions they facilitate, and in the freedom to express those opinions. Yet, in the absence of processes for filtering out some opinions at various stages of policy-making, a maelstrom of different opinions would render governing either impossible or unpredictable. There are two reasons why this kind of diversity poses problems. One is obvious: the greater the differing views and opinions that must be heard and taken account of at each stage of policy-making, the greater the difficulties of co-ordination to reach a final outcome. This is why would-be democracies that generate a multitude of small political parties which are not soon consolidated during democratization often prove unstable. The other problem is that people come to believe that their own opinions are just as good as anyone else's. If they do, they are more likely to persist with their own views and not modify them when encountering those who have more expertise or experience with which to form judgements. In the early 1840s Tocqueville identified this loss of authority in the United States as a potential threat to its society, because:

> Americans are taught from birth that they must overcome life's woes and impediments on their own. Social authority makes them mistrustful and anxious, and they rely upon its power only when they cannot do without it. This first becomes apparent in the schools, where children play by their own rules and punish infractions they define themselves. One encounters the same spirit in all aspects of social life.
>
> *(Tocqueville, 2004, p. 215).*

Essentially, his argument was that authority is accepted only when individuals cannot do without it, and absent these conditions the emergence of authorities or experts is rendered less probable. Instead, people will defer to majority opinion as being legitimate, irrespective of how ill informed it might be. While Tocqueville believed that there were features of American society that could counteract this tendency, the enduring significance of his argument lies elsewhere. It is that he identified the potential danger of egalitarianism for any society where people believe there is none superior to their own views. A society that was fully egalitarian in this way would be potentially unstable.

In the 20th century establishing democracy would depend not just on granting the vote to all adults, but also in there being institutions to filter opinion so that public debate and public policy-making were not chaotic. It was a role played by political parties, trade unions, churches, national media and many others. They helped to prevent the rise of flash movements that could command a majority which was both fragile and ill informed. These institutions could not prevent bad policy-making, something which persists throughout the democratic world, but it could stop "blunders" from being the norm of governmental action. Nor did the existence of "authorities" on issues produce full consensus. Just as experts on art history can disagree as to whether a painting is, or is not, the work of a specific artist, so there are competing views among experts on the viability or desirability of any public policy. As with the art historians, there are many different factors to be considered when forming a judgement, and experts can disagree on the weight to give each of them. To be an authority on some matter, therefore, is not to reach the "best" conclusion all the time, although someone ceases to count as an expert if they fail consistently to reach some minimum standard in their judgements.

One of the main changes in British politics during the past few decades has been the demise of trust in the role of authorities and experts, and, in its place, has emerged a style of public debate that is more akin to the conflict of individual views. Anything goes, and counts equally, however flimsy the arguments or the evidence provided. It is a way of conducting politics that is more egalitarian, because every opinion counts the same. Whether in the long term it can provide for a durable democracy is a different matter. A good illustration of the transformation is to compare the referendum on the Common Market in 1975 with that on the EU in 2016. (This author has "no particular axe to grind" on the substantive issues at stake, having supported the losing side in both referendums – to leave the Common Market in 1975 and to remain in the EU in 2016 – and would still defend both his decisions.)

The two referendums originated from internal divisions in the party calling the referendum, Labour in 1975 and the Conservatives in 2016. On both occasions conducting a general election campaign on a pledge to withdraw would almost certainly have split the governing party badly, such that some members of parliament would have fought an election as independents or founded new parties. In 1975 as well as in 2016, the evidence as to the likely consequences of withdrawal was sparse and uncertain, although most experts on economics and business supported greater economic integration with Europe. Consequently, it is a mistake to view the 1975 contest as one of wholly rational decision-making. As in 2016, there were a plethora of different arguments deployed by different groups. However, the 1975 referendum was primarily held within the bounds of either what was knowable about the likely consequences or at least what was possible. By contrast, the 2016 referendum was characterized on both sides by wild exaggerations, scaremongering and a plethora of different claims, some of which were incompatible with one another. The explanations and judgements of experts played a limited role in the campaign and in forming voting intentions. While it was certainly a decision founded on a certain kind of egalitarian principle, with many and varied opinions propagated in public debate, the outcome scarcely reflected such relevant evidence as there was. Nor would it have done had the Remain side won the vote.

With referendums, and as was the case with Brexit, there is more likely to be chaos in public discussion when there are multiple groups on both sides of the issue on the ballot, each with a somewhat different view or position. The filtering of debate that is usually provided by parties in election contests can be absent in referendums, so that the coherence of what is at stake is less than with an election. Enforcing any rules relating to how campaigns may be conducted, or financed, is far more difficult with the former. Again, because in elections it is organizations, typically parties, at the centre of campaigning, there are usually some informal boundaries within which most operate. This occurs without compromising the rights of individuals to express their views. The absence of such constraints in some referendums is in an obvious sense more egalitarian, but it can be at the expense of effective procedures for democratic decision-making. That is one reason why referendums are best suited to issues that are not multi-dimensional, and where the voters do possess some knowledge of the subject on which they are voting. The orderliness with which the two referendums on the New Zealand flag were conducted in 2015 and 2016 was possible for these reasons, for example. They were conditions wholly absent from the Brexit referendum.

The partial demise of expertise as a factor in shaping public debate extends beyond the Brexit issue; arguably that was merely one of its more extreme and far-reaching manifestations so far. Why has this happened? Why is there less acceptance of authoritative judgement, and a more widespread belief that someone's opinion is no more interesting or valuable than anyone else's? It is a relatively recent development with various causes. They include the demise of many social and political organizations that were central to the filtering of mass opinions, the fragmentation of mass media and the rise of new forms of inter-personal communication, and much greater publicity being given to instances of experts "having got it wrong". Moreover, there is also now a more widespread belief that experts are often not independent, and that they serve their own interests or those of an ultimate paymaster. Certainly institutes, many so-called research centres and similarly named bodies have been funded to counter the dominant orthodoxy on some matters, under the guise that they follow the canons of behaviour that academics were supposed to follow. This merging of the formation of independent judgment with propaganda makes it more difficult for those who were "an authority" on some matter to have their views attended to now.

This plethora of supposed expertise has occurred in an era when public policy is seen widely as having "failed". Slower economic growth since the mid-1970s, the rise of very low paid jobs, an inadequate supply of housing and many other factors have all contributed to the equivalent of shouts directed frequently by irate football crowds against a referee: "you don't know what you're doing". However, unlike televised football games, there are not experts who, by looking at filmed evidence of a controversial incident, can explain why referees may have made the correct decisions, or why they should not be blamed in a particular instance for making a "wrong" one. With public policy it may be decades before vindication of expert judgement is available. Consequently, erosion of confidence in authoritative judgements grows. Furthermore, while consistently poor referees would usually be the ones removed from the panels from which referees are selected, those who exercised good judgement in making policy are often just as likely to be evicted from their positions as those who failed to do so.

Structuring opinion in a democracy

Especially during the Cold War, some political writers used to claim that equality was necessarily in conflict with liberty, and that the latter should prevail. That debate has largely receded. Certainly, like all principles, equality can conflict with others, and how we should resolve those conflicts is subject to disagreement. There are few who would argue that equality should always prevail. In relation to the governing of any body larger than a small community, the key problem with equality is that individual members cannot be fully equal in decision-making, because of their numbers. Equality has to be compromised here, and a failure to do so places strains on governing. Like his contemporary Tocqueville, John Stuart Mill was concerned about how unfiltered opinions might prove a serious weakness for countries founded on some notion of majority rule. He did not:

> question the claim of the majority to "paramount power": "But it is necessary that the institutions of society should make provision for keeping up, in some form or other, as a corrective to partial views, and a shelter for freedom of thought and individuality of character, a perpetual and standing Opposition to the will of the majority".
>
> *(Burns, 1957, pp. 171–172).*

This "Opposition" was social, as much as political, encompassing various institutions and organizations through which alternative views were formed, and indeed these means would emerge in Britain to give structure to the milliard of individual views within it. For about a century and a half this filtering process prevented Mill's underlying fear about majorities from coming close to realization. It is their declining influence in recent decades, and the role now played by social media in facilitating interactions on a massive scale between people not personally known to one another, that has facilitated the rise of more, and varied, "unfiltered" opinions in the political arena. The demise of authorities, in the sense of those with informed views, may well persist and the potential problem identified by Mill re-emerge for British democracy.

It might be argued, however, that this conclusion is too pessimistic – the era of "equality of opinion" has also given rise also to political mobilization by those who would wish to promote various forms of social equality. Unquestionably activism of this kind has developed to counteract anti-egalitarian activism on the political Right, and an engaged citizenry is usually regarded as healthy for a democracy. It has been one of the great resources available to proponents of egalitarian goals, through their ability and willingness to appeal to reasoned argument and to engage in activities promoting them. Particular arguments might not be won, but those participating "live to fight another day" in subsequent ones. The ultimate resolution of conflict via argument depends on some notion of authority – that some considerations are identifiable as being more important than others. It is this which the equality of opinion erodes and is the path to Trumpism and beyond.

When activists turn partly towards direct action in opposing anti-egalitarians the danger to democracy is that it could then move from being a temporary expedient for these activists to becoming a key vehicle in the pursuit of an egalitarian agenda. The more politics moves outside the bounds of confrontations based on reasoning and turned into contests of strength – of mere political power or physical force – the more likely anti-egalitarianism is to triumph. From the revolutions of 1848, to that in Russia in 1905, to the Spanish Civil War (1936–1939) and to Tiananmen Square (1989) this could be said to have happened. Of course, the (first) Russian Revolution of February 1917, or the fall of the Berlin Wall might be cited as counterexamples, but unquestionably egalitarians cannot usually expect to be the winners when reasoned argumentation is diminished as a strategy. Britain, along with other democracies, has now entered a period in which reasoned argument and evidence seems less effective in expanding support for all kinds of egalitarian (and other) aims. The temptation to take on opponents by alternative means – to generate publicity, to goad the opposition into unpopular action or whatever – has become that much greater.

Whilst not violent, throwing milkshakes at anti-egalitarians, as happened to Nigel Farage and Stephen Yaxley-Lennon in 2019, has the potential for similar instances encouraging violence later. Whether this occurs depends on whether a spiral of anger and confrontation has developed over the issues prompting it, and that can happen quickly. The Civil Rights movement began its peaceful campaign in Northern Ireland in early 1967, held its first protest march in 1968 but by late 1969 the armed conflict later known as "The Troubles" had already supplanted it. Although the circumstances in Northern Ireland were unquestionably exceptional, activism that involves physical confrontation with opponents can be explosive in other circumstances too, requiring responses by state agencies that do not exacerbate the underlying conflicts.

Furthermore, in an era of so-called "fake news" it matters much less whether something corresponds to reality, but rather that enough people want to believe that it is true – and for them it then becomes true. Donald Trump retained the support of his core believers for so long because of this; for his supporters it did not matter that what he said was demonstrably untrue, contradictory or the opposite of what he had claimed earlier. Ours is becoming an era of intense partisanship, although not in the sense, as in the United States, that people adhere solidly to a specific political party. Rather, many people now increasingly persist with the views they hold in the face of good reasons as to why they should not hold them. These are not optimal circumstances for those who believe in reducing economic and social inequalities and are seeking to do so.

References

Bartels, Larry M. (2018). *Unequal Democracy: The Political Economy of the New Gilded Age*, 2nd ed. Princeton, NJ: Princeton University Press.

Brady, David, Polsby, Nelson W., and Robinson, Peter (1997). *Campaign Finance: Roll Back the Reforms*. Stanford, CA: Hoover Institution.

Burns, J. H. (1957). "J.S. Mill and Democracy: 1829–61", *Political Studies*, 5, pp. 158–175.

Cadwalladr, Carole (2019). Available at https://www.ted.com/talks/carole_cadwalladr_facebook_s_role_in_brexit_and_the_threat_to_democracy. Accessed 17 April 2019.

Goodwin, Matthew and Heath, Oliver (2016). *The Brexit Vote Explained: Poverty, Low Skills and Lack of Opportunity*. Report of the Joseph Roundtree Foundation, 31 August. Available at https://www.jrf.org.uk/report/brexit-vote-explained-poverty-low-skills-and-lack-opportunities. Accessed 11 February 2018.

Lively, Jack (1975). *Democracy*. Oxford: Blackwell.

Naylor, Robin, Smith, Jeremy, and Telhaj, Shqiponza (2015). *Graduate Returns, Degree Class Premia and Higher Education Expansion in the UK*. London School of Economics, Centre for Economic Performance Working Paper No. 1392.

Page, Benjamin I. and Gilens, Martin (2018). *Democracy in America? What has Gone Wrong and What We Can do About it?* Chicago: University of Chicago Press.

Rix, Kathryn (2008). "The Elimination of Corrupt Practices in British Elections? Reassessing the Impact of the 1883 Corrupt Practices Act", *The English Historical Review*, 123(No. 500), pp. 65–97.

Rokkan, Stein (1966). "Norway: Numerical Democracy and Corporate Pluralism", in Robert A. Dahl (ed.), *Political Opposition in Western Democracies*. New Haven, CT: Yale University Press, pp. 70–115.

Tocqueville, Alexis de (2004). *Democracy in America*. New York, NY: Library of America.

Ware, Alan (2015a). "The Great British Education 'Fraud' of the Twentieth and Twenty-First Centuries", *The Political Quarterly*, 86(4), pp. 475–484.

Ware, Alan (2015b). "Yes, A Fraud", *The Political Quarterly*, 86(4), pp. 489–492.

8

OBSERVATIONS ON FUTURE REDISTRIBUTION IN BRITAIN

In 1920 H. L. Mencken made a remark that spawned many later versions: "there is always a well-known solution to every human problem—neat, plausible, and wrong". Certainly, there have been several supposed remedies for making advanced industrial countries more economically and socially equal which are neat and initially, at least, plausible. Yet, although not all may be "wrong", each has encountered problems in implementation, has generated unwanted consequences or has ceased operating effectively under changed conditions. For example, Marxists sought to replace privately owned capital with community owned and controlled capital, a move that would eliminate the power accruing to private owners. Leninists aimed to achieve the same objective by transferring privately owned capital to the state. In the late 1950s and 1960s Croslandites argued that an economy run on Keynesian lines would grow sufficiently to provide enough resources for state provision of improved social services, thereby benefitting all (Crosland, 1956). This would not yield the full redistribution desired by Marxists or Leninists, but continual improvement and expansion of these services would reduce social inequality. Then there were the Blairites who supported the Labour leader's exhortation of 1996: "Ask me my three main priorities for government and I tell you: education, education and education." Inequality was going to be reduced by increasing educational opportunities for all. Deprived children would not necessarily have to remain deprived in their later years. A more radical solution that would reduce social inequality was a basic income, first discussed widely in the 1990s. The state would provide everyone with a minimum basic income, with supplementation via paid work being optional, so that each person retained freedom of choice about doing so (van Parijs, 1995).

As some subsequent variations on Mencken's original observation stress, there are those who propound neat and plausible solutions to even *complex* problems, and with predictable consequences. Even a basic income for all set at a generous level would solve only some of the problems of social inequality, while less ambitious schemes may fail to generate all the results that it was imagined they could. For instance, Finland's experiment with a targeted basic income for the jobless failed to increase their entry into the labour market (Hiilamo, 2019). No one should doubt that attempting to counteract inequality is a complex issue, with many diverse aspects. To take just one example from recent times, the Labour party proposal for abolishing university tuition fees would provide redistribution in one respect: the generational inequality created this century would be removed. However, it would not deal with the crucial inequality arising from positional competition. Students would still have an incentive to attend the most prestigious universities, and those whose families had had private resources to fund aspects of their earlier education would have a distinct advantage in gaining admission to them. Then, for example, there is the different kind of complexity outlined in Chapter 6, where groups and sub-groups now claim rights to equal treatment and respect when much earlier the problem of inequality had been understood in simple one-dimensional terms involving resources.

In dealing with complexity in public policy, espousing a rather vague "big idea" is useful in rallying public support, but as a guiding principle with which to organize and make compatible the various policies needed it is not. Even more specific "mid-range" ideas, such as using an enhanced inheritance tax to facilitate redistribution for future generations, would counter only some aspects of contemporary inequality in social resources. For instance, it might help shrink the demand for private education whilst doing little to limit the migration of the more affluent to the catchment areas of the better performing schools. Typically politicians are attracted to big ideas, but also both fear and try to disguise policy failures that ensue. The problem for them is that the two may be causally connected. Political ambition and a desire to create policies having electoral appeal can result in their complexity being underestimated, partly because they are implemented too quickly. Consequently, it is their failures that receive lasting publicity, even in cases when a policy might otherwise have been feasible. Universal credit, a flagship policy announced by the former Conservative leader Iain Duncan Smith in 2010, was hailed by the government as simplifying various social benefit payments in ways that it claimed would be fairer to both claimants and taxpayers. From the first stages of its introduction in 2013 it was subjected to many criticisms covering a myriad of failings in its implementation. Policy flagships can become as obsolete as were battleships for navies after the 1940s, and this is especially true of policies relating to inequality. What is required is a wide range of different policies. When particular initiatives fail, as some inevitably will, an approach by government that leads to their quick abandonment and the devising of new approaches is needed. An egalitarian political agenda has to be directed by leadership that is flexible, rather than rigid, in pursuing its goals.

The New Deal is a classic illustration of this point. Roosevelt's pre-election catchphrase "a new deal for the American people" captured public imagination, but the New Deal that his administration inaugurated from March 1933 was anything but a unified approach to resolving the consequences of the Great Depression. It consisted of a whole variety of unrelated programmes, a scattershot approach in which those policies that did not work were quickly abandoned, and other initiatives started. Only some of the New Deal legislation, including the 1935 Social Security Act, produced exceptional long-term beneficial effects. However, overall it is rightly judged as one of the great broad-ranging policy successes of any country in the 20th century. The flexibility in its approach was arguably its major asset.

One important lesson from the New Deal is that to take redistribution seriously entails recognizing that some approaches have major limitations in some contexts, as well as the opportunities they offer in others. Taking that lesson to heart entails for this author his not outlining an agenda here for reducing inequality. That aim is far too ambitious in its scope to conclude a short study that has tried primarily to outline how we got from L. P. Hartley's "foreign country" of the past to the inequalities of today. It would be entirely inappropriate, and misleading, to do so. However, among the many factors, means and limitations relevant to the complications ensuing from the pursuit of greater equality, and the resulting need for flexibility in constructing appropriate policies, are a few discussed briefly below. They illuminate the general point that successful redistribution entails far more than a mere commitment to egalitarianism, but also an understanding of the variations evident in different aspects and contexts of inequality.

Nevertheless, it must first be emphasized that to acknowledge this is certainly not to suggest that countering inequality entails incrementalistic policies. This is most obviously the case in one specific area: preventing unequal treatment for future generations because of environmental damage. Here major policy initiatives are increasingly essential, with many having to be started on a large scale now. One major difference today compared with the experience of earlier generations is that the damage created by air pollution or climate change affects much greater territory, and more people, than the dust bowls or mini ice ages of previous centuries. Humans moving on from damaged environments to others is a solution of diminishing relevance. Without co-ordination both between states and within different policy areas in each state subsequent generations will suffer from unequal treatment by the present generation and its immediate successors. However, the scale of that probable inequality is matched by the complexity of initiating action at a level that might produce success. And, of course, a central problem here is that, while immediate dangers can often prompt effective political action and co-ordination, likely disasters years ahead may continue to be placed, at least partly, on the proverbial backburner by decision-makers.

Elsewhere there are many obvious policies that, if appropriately enacted, could have redistributive consequences. These include various forms of more progressive taxation and changing an emphasis on expanding higher education to a more balanced approach that includes other forms of training for skilled and semi-skilled jobs. The latter could be linked to the revived use of an industrial strategy, an approach abandoned with the adoption of neo-liberal economic policy in the Thatcher governments (Jones, 2018). In part, gathering support for policies that will have egalitarian consequences depends on context: on how successful specific policies are understood as having been in the recent past. Thus, after the 1970s industrial policy was abandoned in Britain, rather than revised, because of the economic turbulence of that decade. However, over time perceptions do change.

Changing interests and social values

One exemplar of this in relation to an egalitarian policy is the National Health Service (NHS). Before its introduction in 1948 both the British Medical Association and many doctors individually opposed the creation of the NHS. While its purpose was to make medical treatment available to all, the medical profession believed its own autonomy and possibly the livelihood of its members, would be adversely affected by the NHS. Within decades that had changed, as newcomers to the profession became socialized into the NHS, understanding its advantages for themselves and patients. While some still wanted the freedom to pursue various aspects of private practice, that was viewed decreasingly by them as an alternative to the NHS. New generations of medical students and doctors became some of its strongest defenders. A very different case, but one similarly involving long-term change in attitudes, was that of public understanding of homosexuality. At the time of its legalization in 1967, support for the legislation derived primarily from the social ills of legal prohibition – including opportunities for blackmailing men. Many of those who backed legal reform wanted to eliminate that, but at the same time did not view the gay community as individuals choosing a lifestyle as valuable as that of heterosexuality. Within decades this situation had been transformed, with widespread acceptance of comparability between lifestyles. Of course, in some social spheres, including among professional footballers and rugby players, as well as those who hold strong religious beliefs, the change has been less evident and overt prejudice persists. However, discrimination against gays and lesbians not only became illegal, but is now widely regarded as appropriately so.

Yet in some contexts, perceptions and values do not change in an egalitarian direction, especially when their own self-interest is entirely obvious to beneficiaries of an inequality. Indeed in some respects anti-egalitarianism is more evident today than previously. Among the affluent, few now seem to view progressive taxation as their fair share of the costs of maintaining social, political and economic structures that make possible their advantages. Instead, they see it merely as an obstacle to be overcome by financial planning and schemes. While many may flinch from using illegal means, there is a far larger group that is determined to protect their own interests to the hilt. The attitude of one of my relatives, whose life spanned nearly all of the 20th century and who, unusually for a woman, had been a successful businessperson in the inter-war years, would now seem archaic to most. A lifetime Conservative, she knew that on her death nearly 40 per cent of the value of her estate would be paid in taxation. She regarded this as fair and an appropriate contribution to society on her part, given her financial circumstances.

In the contemporary era redistribution of capital via taxation involves intricate conflicts between families and their planners, on one side, and tax authorities and legislators on the other. The key feature of their interactions is the persistent and continuing search for advantage by the former, through new schemes and strategies that will preserve legally their private interests. For those whose role is to protect more general interests, there is never a point at which that conflict will finally be won by them. There will always be another round of it.

This is the normal state of affairs when, in the absence of either some notion of obligation to the community or altruism, strong private interests are at stake. For 22 years I was a participant in a contest between private and more general interests, although in a very different arena. As a tutor in an Oxford college I was responsible, with others, for admitting those students who seemed to have the greatest potential for performing well in their studies. Our opponents were teachers, primarily although not exclusively in private sector schools, who wanted to secure advantage for their pupils in the latter's competition with other applicants. Their schools typically had resources that, in various ways, could help their pupils appear to have greater potential than others of similar talent, but who had lesser family and school resources in support of their own abilities. This arose because the success of the former schools and their teachers depended on being seen to get as many pupils as they could into Oxbridge. Ultimately their reputations, and hence maintenance of school income, depended on such outcomes in a market where securing the advantages of an elite higher education had driven parents into paying continually rising school fees. Indirectly, these teachers were simply hired agents, and we were their (paid) opponents. Their role was to find new means of maintaining or creating an advantage for their "clients". Our task was to find ways of neutralizing that, through how we evaluated candidates, aiming to keep the "playing field as level" as we could. Where self-interest is directly at stake the modification or transformation of attitudes and values is improbable, and the continuity of competitive interactions between private and general interests is inevitable. In effect, absent the immediate and complete removal of the former along Leninist lines, the redistribution of prized resources can be successful only if treated as a continuous, dynamic, process by those committed to it.

The roles of markets and the state

Libertarians usually argue that social redistribution is permissible only when it is the result of freely chosen actions – such as via market mechanisms. One significant objection to this claim is that it privileges present consumers over future generations, people who cannot participate in contemporary transactions. For instance, by comparison with the previous generation, the latter's inferior position in the contemporary British housing market was the consequence of actions by public policy makers in which they could not participate. There is no good reason why those who could participate should be privileged in this way, and it provides an obvious justification for protecting the interests of subsequent generations from the self-interest or incompetence of adults alive now. Only the state can provide sufficient safeguards for them, should it choose to do so; markets cannot. In addition, this housing example exposes a further limitation in arguments supporting minimal government.

As we saw in Chapter 5, the current housing shortage was precipitated by the forced demise of public housing providers, who previously, and alongside the private sector, maintained an adequate supply of housing overall. The private sector alone was unable to do so, because of what might be regarded as perverse incentives in the British housing market. It was these incentives that would later produce an inadequate response to demand, and to the generational inequality now being experienced.

Just as the libertarian cannot sustain an argument that redistribution should result only from free choice, so a determined egalitarian cannot claim that markets are necessarily incompatible with greater equality. Governments in a democracy can create, and then maintain, inequality. An extreme example is the history of New York City cab medallions. Their introduction in 1937 by the city government arose as a countermeasure to the over-supply of taxis in the city, one consequence of which had been to depress the incomes of drivers. Only cabs awarded the medallions could tout for business on the streets, and the medallion was granted the status of personal property that, for example, children of an owner could inherit. Subsequently, medallion holders became a powerful political lobby in the city, preventing it from issuing new medallions even when demand for taxis increased greatly. For 60 years no new medallions were issued, and when eventually 2000 new ones were granted it did little to help meet the shortage of cabs on the streets. The sale value of a medallion in the 2010s was about $1,000,000. Here a freer market in more recent decades would have reduced inequality between, on one side, cab drivers who already possessed a medallion and, on the other, those who wanted to drive a cab for a living but lacked the capital to buy one. Both unlimited supply of taxis before 1937 and fixed supply later, sustained by political inaction, had inegalitarian consequences. Markets are not neutral with respect to fair distribution, but neither are they always an anti-egalitarian instrument.

Quotas

Quotas, requiring an organization to select a minimum proportion of appointees from a specific social group, can be a potent device for redistributing power or benefits in some contexts. For example, they have done so in several political parties that established a minimum quota for women as candidates for public office. However, their successes have typically occurred where other factors also facilitated their being effective. Thus, how quotas have helped increase representation for women is complex and has varied (Krook, 2009). The diverging impact of their use here parallels that of other institutional devices used for social redistribution.

A need for quotas typically arises when there are systemic factors or, alternatively, cultural ones strongly favouring the selection of a dominant group, irrespective of the professed support for equality by selectors during recruitment. In the case of candidate selection by parties in advanced economies, there was usually little doubt that many women who could have been selected, but were not, had the required skills and met the criteria for selection. This condition is important in establishing support for quotas. In its absence, selection under quota systems might come to be regarded merely as tokenism, with the subsequent careers of women in politics being limited and the quota system itself subject to criticism.

Quotas were also used after 1907 when scholarships, from elementary schools to an expanded grammar school system, were introduced. Local-authority-funded grammar schools were mandated to set aside a proportion of their places for those awarded scholarships by the authority, with the remaining (fee-paying) pupils being admitted through means chosen by the school. The scheme's principal limitation was that there were so few places available at these schools, that social mobility via the education system was small and that the pool of "talent" reaching the highest levels of the British job market was tiny. Despite this, and of significance for the present argument, is that those selected were no less academically skilled for their age than most of their middle-class fee-paying peers. Moreover, because few middle-class children attended elementary schools, quotas for children there did result in the scholarships largely promoting egalitarian ends – albeit in a small way. In that respect the 11+ regime that replaced it after 1944, and in which scholarships were abandoned, was no more egalitarian. Although the proportion of children at grammar schools increased in that period to 20 per cent of the total, many middle-class children were entitled to take the 11+ examination. Thereby they received a place that might otherwise have been awarded to a working-class child. (In an obvious sense, of course, both regimes were inegalitarian, because the majority of working-class children continued to be excluded from those schools which, for them, were the main routes into middle-class jobs.)

If a class bias in entry to the most skilled jobs today is to be countered, establishing quotas (related to family income) for entry to the most prestigious universities would be an obvious contemporary application of the principle deployed in a different way in schools a century ago. In conjunction with fee levels being both uncapped and set for individual students on the sole basis of parental income, it would be a clearly egalitarian strategy for promoting greater equality of opportunity – at least for those displaying some academic talent as adolescents. But, in at least one important respect, this case is more complicated than the two previously mentioned. Many of those currently excluded, however talented, may not have reached the standard required for starting a demanding university course, because of the quality of the schools they attended. They are not yet the equals of those who have had the advantages of superior schooling. To be effective, and to avoid the social waste of students with previously inadequate training performing poorly at elite universities, pre-university schemes for bridging the gap would have to be introduced in a far more extended way than they have been at present.

In other words, by themselves, formal quotas would probably be insufficient for much improving equality of opportunity in the competition for the most prestigious educational credentials. Are they necessary though? Might it be argued that the two schemes announced by Oxford University in 2019, to ensure that by 2023 one-quarter of its undergraduates were from disadvantaged socioeconomic backgrounds, be a feasible alternative to quotas? Quite possibly for Oxford, with its relatively small undergraduate programme and relatively large resources. Aside from Cambridge, the much larger intakes of other Russell Group universities together with less wealth would preclude them trying to match Oxford's ambitions. Odd cases like Oxford aside, in the absence of formal quotas it is hard to see how the contemporary positional economy of education would do anything except continue to reinforce existing class barriers.

Why redistribution matters

If successful redistribution in the direction of greater equality is a complex and multi-faceted issue, why does it matter? An obvious answer that many would volunteer is that a failure to do is socially unjust. But is this the only answer, and how might one convince those on the Right who reject the significance of social justice as a value that it is one that they too should take seriously?

One reason for them to do so is that new inequalities can, although not invariably, produce protests and social disturbance requiring state response. Suppression can be effective in quelling this – as it was eventually with the Peasant's Revolt in 1381 or with Peterloo in 1819 – but not always. Nor is it cost free. Moreover, in the contemporary era, the speed of communications with others has increased so much that it is far easier for protest to be publicized and mobilized than earlier. Older mechanisms for filtering the variety of opinions emerging within a population are less effective now, so that channelling potential protest in ways that make it more containable has become difficult. Then there is an unfortunate fact about the contemporary era that it succeeds one in which some expectations were more broadly satisfied than they are now. While the truly impoverished may be proportionately fewer than a century ago, there are many other groups who understand their own situation as being inferior to those of their predecessors.

This is why Franklin Roosevelt is a much better model of political leadership for conservatives today than is, say, Margaret Thatcher. Clearly, for progressives, the importance of Roosevelt is that the New Deal exposed *how* to approach complex policy problems with some success. By contrast, for conservatives, his relevance is that social redistribution is not an issue to be monopolized by those well to the left of the political centre ground, and who have egalitarian views. Roosevelt was not an extreme egalitarian. Indeed, most notably he did not take any initiatives whatsoever towards reducing, let alone eliminating, racial segregation in the southern states. (That political minefield would be confronted for the first time in the 20th century by his immediate successor, Harry Truman.) Yet he recognized that the situation he inherited in March 1933 of America being, in Will Rogers' words, "the only nation in the history of the world that ever went to the poor house in an automobile", required policies that directly or indirectly would have egalitarian consequences. Thus, one mainstream interpretation of Roosevelt is that he was the saviour of American capitalism, and not some kind of proto-socialist (Lipset and Marks, 2000, 2001). Roosevelt was the consummate politician, changing his public stances as necessary on issues, which, for example, he had done several times on prohibition between 1927 and 1933 (Ware, 2006, pp. 161–162). For him, it was what was needed in specific circumstances that drove what he said and did. Politics as usual often does not work and can be dangerous when there is the potential for social discontent to prompt direct political action – whether from the Left or the Right, or anywhere else. The problems posed by inegalitarianism and its causes today are certainly not as immediate or critical as they were in early 1930s America, but they are quite likely to constitute a continuing chronic condition facing British governments well into the future.

The potential for social and political instability is not the only reason for an anti-egalitarian to view rising levels of inequality with some foreboding. Its consequences can adversely affect others in society, imposing various kinds of costs on them. Inequality can prove expensive in several ways. An obvious historical instance of this, and one that even those on the far Right could not dismiss as a mere stalking horse for socialism, involved British army recruitment during the Boer war. It became widely accepted both within the army and among politicians that perhaps only 40 per cent of those seeking to enlist were physically fit enough for active service (Gilbert, 1965, p. 145). These revelations sparked off a national debate about "deterioration", which was widely accepted as being caused by the conditions in which the working class was living. While that aspect of deprivation did change over time, more recently attention has been focussed on other social costs imposed by inequality. Some were highlighted in a well-publicized book published a few years ago (Wilkinson and Pickett, 2009). The authors argued that various social goods – greater social trust, lower incarceration levels and lower levels of regular drug taking included – were more present in societies exhibiting greater equality. Inevitably, perhaps, the study attracted various criticisms, including whether the countries they chose to include were typical, whether race rather than poverty *per se* was an important intervening factor and whether the direction of causation they posited might be incorrect. (Does greater equality cause changes in cultural factors, or might changes in cultural factors prompt greater equality?) Nevertheless, if these points are left on one side, there undoubtedly remains plausibility to the argument that high levels of inequality do have adverse consequences for those other than the people directly suffering from it.

To take an obvious example, people in poor communities more typically smoke cigarettes, use drugs regularly and eat food that is not nutritious. This type of consumption increases the likelihood of their requiring medical treatment and social care when they are older; its costs will be borne by the state, which in turn, via taxation, is funded partly by those who are better off. Although it is the latter who are more likely to experience greater longevity, the population overall has been ageing, and probably more poor people will be living for longer than their predecessors. To the extent that they are experiencing better health, having had healthier lifestyles, the less they will cost future taxpayers.

Obviously, the type of consumption by the poor that worsens health in old age is not chosen, in some kind of rational calculation on their part, but rather is a reflection of common practices, together with high price levels, in their neighbourhoods. Until now hardly anyone in contemporary society believed that those who then suffer the effects of that consumption should be treated as if it had been wilful or an entirely free choice. Any claims from the fringes of the far Right that it was, and that the poor should either themselves bear most of its associated costs or be abandoned, were widely dismissed as wholly unacceptable. More recently, though, stigmatizing the behaviour of an underclass has come back into fashion on the Right, on issues such as obesity and smoking. Yet, if you want to reduce the social costs associated with such behaviour in the long term, then appeals to self-help are as likely to be as effective as they were over poverty in the mid-19th century. In the case of obesity, for instance, alternative foods and drinks may not be readily available in poor neighbourhoods or cost more when they are. Only when that is changed can choice be available. Investing in changing the culture of poverty now makes just as much sense as improving Britons' physical fitness, and hence aspects of their health, did for the British military over a century ago.

Those with progressive political views on social inequality might object to the preceding discussion, because for them it is the social injustice of this inequality that really matters currently, and for the future. The ability of the less affluent to shape their lives, and those of their children, is greatly curtailed by comparison with those who are not, especially the very affluent. That is inherently unjust. However, the point of concluding this book as I have is not to devalue the idea of social justice, but to emphasize that the problems posed by inequality should be significant, too, for a much broader group of people than those who want to minimize social injustice. Countering many aspects of inequality is not just a moral imperative, but is central to practical politics in the 21st century. In many respects, persisting inequality will constrain severely how societies, including Britain's, can even function in decades to come.

Are Britain's political parties up to the task?

As the institutions from which all British governments are formed, political parties would seem crucial to confronting this challenge. Unfortunately, even leaving aside the massive internal conflicts in both major parties that Brexit generated, there are good reasons for believing that many aspects of inequality will not be acted on, or will be ignored or concealed beneath rhetoric supposedly egalitarian in intention.

One obvious reason is the complex nature of inequality today compared with how it operated and was understood until the latter part of the 20th century. Before then, under a two-party system and with a widely accepted uni-dimensional view of inequality, there was an obvious fit between that system and the issue of equality.

Broadly, there was a balance between a Labour party committed to a more egalitarian agenda and a Conservative party that wanted to defend key features of the status quo. Inequality mapped directly onto the British party system. The subsequent rise of other parties – Liberal Democrats, the Scottish National Party (and possibly in the future a Brexit-based party too) – has done little to change a fundamental feature of the earlier era. The aims and policies of the two large parties continue to be shaped by strategies directed at their principal opponent.

In the contemporary era these parties are grappling with egalitarian aims and demands that are multi-faceted, and which do not fit easily into a two-party model. They include those of former Labour voters in the north of England, angry about their relative impoverishment and who now support a Brexit-based party in some elections. Many are expressing a demand for more equal treatment that would not be straightforward for any party to then connect to, say, pressures for LGBT rights or counteracting climate change on behalf of our successors. Building social coalitions based on egalitarian aims is therefore more difficult in the 21st century. Moreover, the constitutional and political structures that kept two parties dominant for so long, including the electoral system, continue to shape how elite politics operates. Truly multi-party politics has not emerged in Britain, so the required flexibility needed for connecting egalitarian aims to the party system, by strategies other than through partisan opposition, is absent. Because the main parties still shape their objectives and policies in relation to what they believe their opponents will do, innovation in constructing large social coalitions, as well as policies, is restricted. This limitation of the British party system was illustrated all too clearly during the extended Brexit saga.

Then there is the point made earlier in this book: according equal treatment now to future generations is hampered by their absence from the current electorate. While some parties do give weight to their interests and likely concerns, many voters can be mobilized in opposition to them because of their beliefs, quite possibly correct ones, that their own interests will be affected adversely. This logic of electoral competition has tended to depress the weight that should be given by parties to a significant element of an egalitarian agenda.

However, there is a still more important consideration. Like all major parties, Britain's are structures established by previous generations. Both their history and their subsequent development make them slow to adapt to new circumstances and demands. Consequently,

> party change does not "just happen". In fact, decisions to change a party's organization, issue positions or strategy face a wall of resistance common to large organizations.
>
> *(Harmel and Janda, 1994, p. 261).*

Typically parties adapt more slowly than is necessary to deal effectively with changed circumstances (Ware, 2009, p. 21). To take one example of the tendency under new conditions to cling to earlier aims and policies, the rise of positional competition to obtain educational credentials from elite institutions, as the main route into the upper sectors of the labour market, is still largely unacknowledged by parties. This occurs despite its consequences being long evident. Instead, the resulting outcomes are often publicized by politicians as the responsibility of various organizations in British society who should deal with their own shortcomings. Thus, they are often accused of not having appropriate procedures to ensure that fewer privately educated people and fewer Oxbridge graduates are recruited, and that more women and racial minorities are hired. That there is a fundamental systemic problem – one deriving from changed incentives in British society and in its economy – is not discussed or publicized in political debate.

Nor are effective policies to counteract it considered. Instead, many would-be egalitarians propose, for example, reducing or eliminating all university tuition fees as a way of benefitting those had been socially disadvantaged. One result of doing so would be to increase the resources available to the affluent, enabling them earlier in the education system to improve their children's prospects in the race to the best jobs. Money not required later for university tuition fees could be spent in various ways to supplement a child's performance during primary or secondary education. By 2019 the Labour party, seeming to recognize that the kind of advantages the affluent had were a major barrier to social mobility, abandoned it as a policy goal. In its place Jeremy Corbyn outlined an anodyne objective that was going to make sure "all of our children achieve their best in school" (*Guardian* 8 June 2019). It was an evasion that conveniently ignored its crucial limitation that, even were every child to achieve the best they could, for each of them future prospects would still largely depend on how they had performed *in relation* to others. With respect to reducing inequality, grasping the proverbial nettle is not something parties want to do, and especially in two party systems.

These persisting weaknesses in Britain's parties and its party system have been complemented more recently by another development: when in government, parties now make less use of non-partisan procedures for examining complex and potentially contentious policies. Until the latter 20th century major policy issues could be handed over by governments to Royal Commissions (and other specially established governmental procedures) to examine, and then report on, the matter. Partly their role was to remove complex policy issues from the highly oppositional mode of British party politics. It is worth remembering that much of the post-war Labour government's social agenda had its origins in, and derived some of its legitimacy from, the Beveridge Report. It was a classic example of that approach. While there are still some instances of it today – the Turner Reports on Pensions earlier this century being one – there is a much-reduced role for this non-partisan mode of policy-making. The result is that the very weaknesses of the parties, in innovating policies, are now less likely to be overcome by the use of other processes and approaches.

I recognize that the concluding observation in this book is highly pessimistic, but I would defend it firmly. Certainly, in public debate the idea of equality is taken more seriously this century than it used to be, and various aspects of unequal practices and behaviour attract widespread public condemnation when they did not previously. Nevertheless, inequality has risen in many key respects and many forms of inequality will surely continue to increase. Often attitudes towards equality are NMBYism writ large – we may want it, but not if it is at our own expense. With political parties being institutions that are inherently slow to innovate, this seems a recipe for continuing popular discontent. For many of my generation, one that benefitted from the modest egalitarianism of the post-1945 political era, it is a development that is both disappointing and worrying. For us, the ancient Chinese curse appears to have been manifested: we are now living in interesting times.

References

Crosland, Anthony (1956). *The Future of Socialism*. London: Jonathan Cape.

Gilbert, Bentley B. (1965). "Health and Politics: The British Physical Deterioration Report of 1904", *Bulletin of the History of Medicine*, 39(March–April), pp. 143–153.

Harmel, Robert and Janda, Kenneth (1994). "An Integrated Theory of Party Goals and Party Change", *Journal of Theoretical Politics*, 6(3), pp. 259–287.

Hiilamo, Heikki (2019). *Disappointing Results from the Finnish Basic Income Experiment*. University of Helsinki, 8 February. Available at https://www.helsinki.fi/en/news/nordic-welfare-news/heikki-hiilamo-disappointing-results-from-the-finnish-basic-income-experiment. Accessed 24 February 2019.

Jones, Richard (2018). "The Second Coming of UK Industrial Strategy", *Issues in Science and Technology*, 34(Winter). Available at https://issues.org/the-second-coming-of-uk-industrial-strategy/ Accessed 5 April 2019.

Krook, Mona Lena (2009). *Quotas for Women in Politics: Gender and Candidate Selection Reform Worldwide*. New York, NY: Oxford University Press.

Lipset, Seymour Martin and Marks, Gary (2000). *It Didn't Happen Here: Why Socialism Failed in the United States*. New York, NY and London: W.W. Norton.

Lipset, Seymour Martin and Marks, Gary (2001). "How FDR Saved Capitalism", *Hoover Digest*, No. 1, 30 January.

van Parijs, Philippe (1995). *Real Freedom for All: What (If Anything) Can Justify Capitalism?* Oxford: Oxford University Press.

Ware, Alan (2006). *The Democratic Party Heads North, 1877–1962*. Cambridge: Cambridge University Press.

Ware, Alan (2009). *The Dynamics of Two-Party Politics: Party Structures and the Management of Competition*. Oxford: Oxford University Press.

Wilkinson, Richard and Pickett, Kate (2009). *The Spirit Level: Why Equality is Better for Everyone*. London: Allen Lane.

INDEX

Note: Page numbers followed by "n" denote endnotes and bold represent tables.